OBAMUNISM
The Enemy Within

By Ed Kugler

GOD SAVE OUR COUNTRY

Ed Kugler

Dedication

My work is dedicated to my four grandchildren.

- Barrett Vance aka: The Bear
- Beckett Vance aka: Beckster the Rockstar
- Carson Vance aka: He's just Carson
- Cameron Kugler aka: Cami

I also dedicate it to all children and grandchildren here in the US and throughout the world. May we return America to its rightful place of leadership and freedom in the world. We owe it to them!

Special Thanks

My work would not have been possible without the help of the following people:

- Robert Fraser for his editing and historical context and advice.
- Steve Alexander for his incredible creativity and graphics work on the cover.
- Gloria Kugler my wife and soul mate.
- To my forty special friends who gave their feedback and advice on the name of this book.

Thank you all for your significant contribution to a very important work. May we make a difference.

Contents

"It is impossible to rightly govern a nation, without God and the Bible."

George Washington

Other Books by Ed Kugler

Dead Center
A Marine Snipers Two-Year Odyssey in the Vietnam War

Poems of a Rogue

My Vietnam

A Dozen Things I Learned About Life
As a Marine Sniper

Through the Darkness Comes the Light

Pocket Change

How to Cope When Your Organization
Is Changing Faster than You Are

Loose Change

The Well House

"If ever time should come, when vain and aspiring men
shall possess the highest seats in Government,
our country will stand in need of its experienced
patriots to prevent its ruin."

Samuel Adams

Foreword

Freedom is not free and liberty never comes without sacrifice. I can personally testify, as a member of the Polish Underground Army, fighting the Nazi regime during the fall of 1944, that the cost of freedom is great and the toll in human sacrifice beyond comprehension. I can also testify that freedom's reward is undoubtedly worth the struggle. Further testimony to our American struggle for freedom, is manifest by the thousands of American GI graves spread across Afghanistan, Africa, Europe, the Middle East, and the Pacific Islands, at the Pentagon and in New York City.

Everywhere we go today, a person, a government or a tyrant wants to vanquish the American dream and replace it with what they believe is a better interpretation of what they think is best for each of us. If we are not willing to fight for our unalienable rights, we will lose them and the enemies of liberty will prevail. A Polish guerrilla leader was once asked what he would do if the comrades, meaning the Russian communists, took over the government of his country. He thought for a moment, and then responded, "Start fighting against the new regime!" He made that statement after four years of fighting German oppression. Our struggle for liberty takes many forms. Many threats are overt and some are clear while the most intransigent of those threats, are those that begin small and become intertwined within the fabric of our society.

In *Obamunism – The Enemy Within,* Ed Kugler identifies the same problem in today's society that I experienced over 60 years ago in Poland. People who have personally known the fear of death, as Ed did in Vietnam, have a profound understanding of human nature and the value of life and sincerity.

When Ed listens to speeches designed to mislead, manipulate, distort the facts or falsify evidence in order to induce the citizens to react in a manner not corresponding with national interest – Ed reacts. His reaction, to the bending of our national interests, is eloquently presented in this book. Regardless of his own political viewpoints, Ed presents his case in a clear and concise manner, leaving the reader to make their own determination based on facts. Mr. Kugler's use of a reasoned approach, to our country's current crisis, is well documented and accurately presented.

As terrorism progressively rears its ugly head, whether in New York, Bali, Somalia, Berlin or Tel Aviv, the entire world witnesses the suffering. The misguided people in our country, who call themselves "occupiers", trample on the freedom of other citizens in the name of the 99%. Yet, we as a citizenry watch the occupiers trample the rights of citizens while our elected officials exhort them in the name of free speech. Obama acknowledged the Occupy protest movement by saying: "You are the reason I ran for office."

Is this the beginning of the tacit acceptance of a group of people to infringe upon the rights of others? Allow me to quote a part of pre-sentencing address of the Shoe Bomber by Judge William Young U.S. District Court: "You are a terrorist. You are not a soldier. It seems to me you hate the one thing that is most precious. You hate our freedom, our individual freedom to live as we choose, to come and go as we choose, to believe or not believe as we individually choose. Here, in this society, the very winds carry freedom. They carry it everywhere from sea to shining sea. It is because we prize individual freedom so much that you are here in this beautiful courtroom." I witnessed the birth of this same type of "occupy" movement, on a smaller scale in 1930's Europe, all in the name of the greater good and redistribution of resources.

Ed Kugler clearly demonstrates his sincere commitment to basic human rights. His devotion and loyalty to nonviolence calls for and advises for us a peaceful metamorphosis, the return to America as our ancestors knew it. Ed has a keen awareness of the political injustices within society and has the courage to speak out against it. He advocates a return to the freedom and democracy from which our country was born – the freedom to succeed or fail, without government intrusion. He notes that the re-distribution of wealth and other failed socialistic-liberal agendas do not fit into American society. Ed has risen to this new challenge, as he did in the jungles of Vietnam, but this time, he is involved as an educator, role model, patriot and peacemaker. Ed Kugler challenges the reader in the same way that he has challenged himself.

Today, our young men and women are willing to sign up, to defend our freedoms, always with the possibility that one day they may be called upon to pay the ultimate sacrifice. Nowhere else in the world, is this 'volunteer force' the cornerstone of a nation's defense. These 'volunteers' are not fighting to preserve 'hope and change.' We were not fighting to preserve 'hope and change' in 1944 Warsaw either. We were fighting to preserve those unalienable rights endowed by our Creator beginning with freedom. Let's not squander our liberty for empty political slogans such as 'hope and change'.

In his previous book, *Dead Center – A Marine Snipers Two Year Odyssey in the Vietnam War,* Ed used language and terminology that was very expressive and self explanatory. He does so in this book as well. Mr. Kugler has proved his competence in dealing with political and social issues. Someone once said, "Heroes are real people, not perfect, not infallible, not immortal, but nevertheless constructive role models." Ed Kugler is one of them.

I especially like the way Arthur Ashe defines what it means to be a hero. He said, "True heroism is remarkably sober, very undramatic. It is not the urge to surpass all others at whatever cost, but the urge to serve others at whatever cost." Our country needs men like Ed Kugler and books like *Obamunism*. They're not perfect, but they're true to the core beliefs and disciplines that made America great.

It is the adherence to those unalienable rights by people committed to America which have made our country great. Look at the former Soviet Empire. The Soviets planned and managed every aspect of the lives of millions of people. Did they succeed? Those small private patches of ground, in Poland, Hungary, Czechoslovakia and other countries where people could grow their own crops thrived. Eventually, it was the Soviets inability to quell the peoples thirst for freedom that did them in. It started with the Polish people's desire for the freedom of religion. Haven't we learned from the failures of history in the last century? It is only by allowing a free people to pursue their individual goals, that a country becomes strong.

Yet, with billions of dollars of government stimulus, our real unemployment rate remains at 16% and we have lost the respect of countries throughout the world. What has hope and change delivered? In our new war against the terrorists and different "isms", we are waging a two-front war. One against radical Islam and a second-front at home against the backers of class warfare. The loss of freedom can come head on, or, through a slow and methodical degradation of our unalienable rights.

I was witness to the onslaught of "freedom's loss" through tyranny and violence. At least I knew where to look and who to fight. In the fight against the slow degradation of our rights, who do we fight?

Who do we point our fingers to as the executioner of our liberties? It is a much harder and protracted offensive but make no mistake, it is a war that we can easily loose. As free Americans, we must show courage, patriotism and devotion to our country.

Ed's personal experience, as well as his knowledge of the meaning of freedom, determination, oppression, success, failure, foresight, aspiration, and a love of country, he provides the reader an ability to grasp our country's current predicament, downward slide and loss of individuality. He has a distinct no BS manner and offers practical solutions. Ed's patriotism and commitment to truth has been a cornerstone of his life regardless of the price he paid for what he believed in.

We must understand our enemy cannot be trusted. Warsaw, Poland appeared to present the last major obstacle to the Soviet army's triumphant march from Moscow to Berlin. When the German Wehrmacht was pushed back to the Vistula River which divided the city into two parts, we believed that liberation was at hand. So, too, did the Western leaders. We believed that because Soviet radio was calling on Poles to start the 'uprising' for a long period of time before August 1944.

On August 1, 1944, when the Soviet Armies were at the gates of Warsaw, the Polish Underground Army started an Uprising against the German occupation of Warsaw 'hoping' that the Russians would enter the city and help with our 'uprising'.. We Poles forgot that, "Hope is a fool's paradise" (Paraphrased from The Paston Letters, 1462).

The Polish Resistance poured forty thousand plus armed fighters into the streets to drive out the hated Germans. Unfortunately, this action did not coincide with Stalin's master plan for post-war Europe. While the Western Allies were making all possible efforts to win the war against Hitler's armies, Stalin was setting up his plan for control of post-war Eastern Europe.

Stalin condemned our 'uprising' as a criminal adventure and refused to cooperate in assisting Warsaw's freedom fighters. It was simple. It interfered with his plan for post-war Europe.

Keep in mind that just eight months before the uprising, Soviet government radio was calling on the Polish Underground to rise up with their implied support. However, Stalin's most likely purpose was for the Polish Underground to be decimated by the very strong German Army. The sudden stop of Soviet progress at the gate of Warsaw allowed Hitler enough time to order the city of Warsaw and its inhabitants to be annihilated without any mercy. The tragic results indicate that the SS followed Hitler's and Himmler's orders to the letter. Bear in mind that the Uprising was originally planned to last no more than three to four days - just enough time to allow the Russian Army, to cross the Vistula river that divides the city thus having the chance to push towards Berlin. No other natural obstacles existed. But Stalin had other plans.

Today's enemy has no morals, loyalty or commitment to freedom. They are just like the enemy I fought so long ago. There is no doubt that Stalin purposely delayed capturing Warsaw. Providing victory to the Polish Underground was not in Stalin's plan even at the cost of his own soldiers' lives. Did the communists care about the 300,000 casualties that Warsaw suffered – no?

But the communists of old aren't the same today. They learned valuable lessons from their experience. If fundamental revolutionary change, change such as I experienced, were to take place in America, it would require countless lives to be lost. But how many lives would be lost through the slow degradation of our individual liberties? Who would we fight? Would we fight or would we just acquiesce in the name of political correctness?

It would seem impossible that we would ever experience the type of class warfare that was imposed upon my native country by the Soviets. Yet I cannot forget that America and England turned a blind eye to the evidence of the systematic elimination of an entire class of Polish officers, Polish intelligentsia, landowners, and factory owner's, officials and priests at Katyn Forest. The number of victims is estimated at about 22,000. It can and did happen.

We must consider what is being suggested today, by our President when he talks of redistribution of wealth and government control of every aspect of our lives – does it differ from the former Soviet policies? Socialists no longer call themselves socialists. They are disguised under the banner of progressives. Their political philosophy did not change; they just have a new modus operandi. We must wake up!

In *Obamunism* Ed Kugler identifies the 'enemy within'. He was a Marine Sniper fighting for two consecutive years in the Vietnam War. He fought a well camouflaged 'invisible' enemy that was hiding amongst the population in villages and hamlets. He has indentified a new, old enemy within. Ed suffered injuries and was decorated and never lost his love for his country.

Life was not easy for Ed Kugler, but these tough times taught him many lessons, and hardened his determination to succeed. Conditions in Vietnam were very difficult, just as they are in today's war in Afghanistan. Ed wrote in *Dead Center*, "When you are in the death business, each dawn could be your last." In spite of all that, Ed learned to skillfully separate fact and fiction.

I am glad Mr. Kugler made it and wrote *Obamunism-The Enemy Within*. We live in the most beautiful country in the world. Until recently we lived under a constitutional government. Are we perfect, of course not, humans are not perfect, but as a country we are an example to the world.

No other country has ever been such a magnet to immigrants as America was and still is. People living under Communist regimes continue to risk their lives to come to America. We should remember the Berlin Wall and how many Germans risked their lives to escape to the Western Sector.

There was and is only one reason, to be free. Fellow Americans, our country is not perfect but it is the best in the world. *I have lived under the German occupation and felt the brunt of their brutality, violence and viciousness - our lives had no value – we were the subject of execution any time any German decided. Allow me to be a little sentimental and let me conclude paraphrasing something I read some time ago, but do not remember the source, being a senior citizen, at times, my memory is not what it used to be. According to the American Heritage Dictionary the word grateful means: appreciative; thankful; expressing gratitude; pleasing; agreeable.*

In my heart the deep meaning of grateful is remembering and being very thankful, for the little and special blessings in my life. I never take for granted the simple blessings like being alive, having a great family and being a free American. America is a very special country. I am grateful to live in America. I lost my freedom once. I do not take my freedom in America for granted; I respect it and am grateful for it. Consider the following:

1. I am most grateful every day because I am reminded that I am alive and living in a free country.

2. I am grateful that I can become what I aspire to be and practice my beliefs freely. I am healthy and happy and thankful for all of God's blessings.

There is an appropriate Latin proverb, *"Audaces fortuna iuvat"*. The translation reads, "Fortune favors the brave (or bold)". Ed Kugler is a brave man who wrote his book *"Obamunism -The Enemy Within"* for the benefit of all Americans. He wrote it bravely and boldly. There is never a question what Ed Kugler wishes to say. He is a Marine through and through – a true man that is part of a vanishing breed.

My advice to all of my fellow citizens is to read it and take it to heart. We need to love, protect and honor America. We must be proud to be citizens of this beautiful country while we remain committed to its freedom forever. God Bless America!

Stanley Rozycki
Jacksonville, FL

*"We are a nation that has a government,
not the other way around."*

President Ronald Reagan

A Message to America

Stop! Wake up America! Put down your lattes, quit hitting snooze, turn off the TV and get dressed. You'd better be ready, the enemy has been located. He is within. He doesn't have a suicide vest or an AK. He speaks with a teleprompter full of words from the radicals he has surrounded himself with. His name is Barrack Hussein Obama and he doesn't believe Ronald Reagan's words from the quote above.

Let's get right to the point. We have a guy in the White House who is intentionally, as part of 'his' change plan, driving us to the brink of destruction. His actions dovetail with those of enemies passed. He is a dangerous man.

Whether you're a Democrat, Republican, Liberal, Libertarian, Right, Left, Gay, Straight or don't give a big one, I don't care. You can't ignore the fact that our once great Nation is in deep trouble. For once, we need to set aside our partisan politics and special interest groups and do what is right for our Nation by taking a very, very close look at the guy we made our President.

We're in the deepest trouble since our brilliant Founding Fathers conceived of what has become known as the American Dream. As I write this, the American Dream is breathing its last breath because we're asleep at the wheel. We elected a Socialist President. If you want the America millions of people gave their lives for, the one you've enjoyed all your life, the time is now. We must vote the self-anointed one out of office in 2012.

Who am I to be upset? Who am I to call you to action? I'm just an ordinary citizen. I'm a product of the 60's. Born and raised in a small Ohio town, rural America at its best. I grew up amidst the shadow of bomb shelters, hide under your desk drills and the impending battle with Russia.

In our small town we celebrated Memorial Day at the local cemetery that had residents who dated back to the Civil War. I grew up believing in the good of people, love of country and most of all, supporting our government. I knew I lived in the greatest nation on earth. I still do.

Two weeks after high school I joined the United States Marine Corps. In less than a year we were in combat in Santo Domingo, Dominican Republic where I was wounded. I was scared stiff but still committed to my country. The beginning of 1966, I again left this great country to serve in the Vietnam War. I'd return after two years in the war to a foreign country, the United States of America. I couldn't imagine what had happened? That was real change. The book you're reading was inspired by my love for America. After careful research and observation, I know it is heading for a crash, and fast.

In my life there has never been a time like we Americans are living right now. Imagine my surprise after traveling to Canada for three months and returning to headlines such as the following:

1. "New Jersey Teacher being persecuted for being a Christian on her own Facebook page".

2. "Christians Murdered in Egypt by rioters and Egyptian troops".

3. "Tea Party event cancelled at the Hyatt because they are intimidated by the Council on American-Islamic Relations (CAIR)".

4. "Qadafi is killed in Libya".

5. "Texas school children are forced to memorize and recite the Mexican National Anthem and their Pledge of Allegiance in Spanish".

6. "California passes a new law allowing children 12 and up to have sex, be treated for STD's and receive hospital care without parental consent".

7. "The Vice President of the United States proclaims that if we don't pass the President's latest economic package there will be more rapes and murders in the street."

8. "Surprising protests spring up in New York City. Occupy Wall Street rolls across America."

9. "Occupy Orlando protests linked to Hamas and the Muslim Brotherhood".

10. "President Obama declares our borders are safer than ever".

For a minute I thought I was in a time warp. I saw Yogi Berra saying, "Its déjà vu all over again". It isn't 1968, but key dissidents from the 60's infiltrated our government under the 'change umbrella' of Barack Obama and we can see their influence. Obama is the new, pretty face of socialism. We live in very, very dangerous times. Our country is being taken over from the inside by Obama and his revolutionaries with a little help from our one world government friends around the world. If you think those Occupy Wall Street protests just happened ... think again!

We as American citizens have been numbed by our success. We have few people left who remember or have relatives alive from the Great Depression, or the devastation of World War I or even World War II.

We've become a people drunk with credit to buy more things we don't need. We buy houses we can't afford and blame all of it on someone else. Our great Nation was founded on solid principles; personal responsibility was one of them. That's gone, along with our credit rating.

For those of you who disagree, slow down, relax and read on, give truth a chance. For one, I didn't start out disliking this guy. In fact, I thought he might be as good as he thinks he is. My three children wondered that too, and that made me think. I remember seeing him give an address at the Democratic Convention in 2004. I remember being impressed. I thought his guy just might be the bright new face on a political horizon that sorely needed one. His speech was impressive.

I didn't think much about him after the Convention. Like most of you, I dread the Presidential Campaigns and don't pay attention until near Election Day. When he showed up on the scene of the 2008 elections, I figured he deserved a closer look. My kids were still debating and eventually two of the three chose to support Mr. Obama. I watched his speeches, listened to the news and tried really hard to buy into the change he was selling. I really wanted to be a supporter. I spent three months pouring over everything I could find on this guy. I wanted to know what the attraction and change really was.

The more I learned and listened the more fearful I became. In my work life I spent over three decades in leadership positions from the battlefields of Vietnam to the Corporate Boardroom. It's easy to see a talking suit compared to a genuine leader. The dots just didn't connect with me for Obama. At the time, I didn't see him as the threat he turns out to be. I saw him simply as a pretty guy in a suit with lots of money behind him who spoke well. I couldn't miss the fact that he was totally unqualified to run a McDonalds, let alone be President of the United States.

I didn't start out an Obama critic, but his actions don't lie. By observing him and researching extensively over the past year, the picture became clearer. Results come from actions; actions come from behaviors; and behaviors come from thoughts. There is a saying which goes, "What we do every day is what we believe - all the rest is just talk". Mr. Obama is a great speaker. But listen and observe, not just his words, but his actions since taking office. There is something very sinister with Mr. Barack Hussein Obama.

Mr. Obama, surrounded by his band of Socialists, is asking for four more years. If you want the America of old, the country that is the sole reason any democracy exists in this world ... then Obama must go, now! He's taking us down a road to socialism, a road to a one world government and a world where Islam reigns supreme. It sounds crazy, I know. I'm just an average American like you. I also have common sense. You do too! You need to start using it right now by reading this book cover to cover.

We spent three months in our cottage in Canada this summer. The cottage had been in my family for over 50 years. My children grew up going every summer. We were blessed. It was home to them since we moved fifteen times during my work years. My grandchildren have now been enjoying it for seven years. Yet, my wife and I sold it this summer. It was a painful, unpopular family decision. Why did I sell it? First, it has become a burden financially; secondly, I am so concerned about where this country is headed I wanted the money in my hands while I could still get it.

In the scheme of life, my loss is simply sentimental. It doesn't compare to the losses many of you have felt over the past three years of Mr. Obama. I know bright young guys who worked for me at one time and are now out of work, some two and three years. I know more and more people who have lost their homes. That is a first for me. That is not America. It's time to stand up, be counted and make a change for America.

My challenge to each of you is to read this book, mark it up and become familiar with its contents. You must understand the challenge we face. Read it and understand why I could not support what Obama truly represents. Read through it and understand my journey and reasoning for writing this book. Our President is an imposter. He is not our hope for a new America, not the America that has led the world. He wants America to align to his vision of a Socialist world order. I know that is where we are headed.

I want the America I fought for and you will too when you understand the depths of our fall. Read on and you will see the truths so many Americans don't understand or are too busy to see. America remains the greatest nation on earth. It is the world's only beacon of freedom. The time to stand up for America is right now!

In the following chapters, my goal is to raise your blood pressure and piss you off enough that you will take action. We must not reelect this man for another term. The election coming in 2012 is the most important election the Nation has ever faced.

My challenge is from one citizen to another. You must take the blinders off and see what's really coming. Your vote in 2012 will matter more than at any other time in our Nation's history. When you're convinced where we are headed and the changes we need ... convince at least one other person and challenge them to do the same. The time to right the wrongs of America begins right now! It's now, or never.

I love this country. I want it for my children, grandchildren and beyond. I know you do too. It's time to stop being a spectator and get involved in saving America. We're either part of the solution or part of the problem. The choice is yours. If you're part of the solution then choose to do what's right. Choose what's right for America. Choose right now to do your part. Read on!

*"We face a hostile ideology (communism):
global in scope, atheistic in character, ruthless in purpose,
and insidious in method"*

President Dwight D. Eisenhower

"I consider the foundation of the Constitution as laid on this ground: That 'all powers not delegated to the United States, by the Constitution, nor prohibited by it to the States, are reserved to the States or to the people' (10th Amendment). To take a single step beyond the boundaries thus specifically drawn around the powers of Congress, is to take possession of a boundless field of power, no longer susceptible to any definition."

Thomas Jefferson

A Brief Look at America's Enemy

We in America have always had enemies. Why? Because we are the first and only beacon of freedom the world has ever seen. We have a few satellite countries that enjoy freedom under our umbrella of safety. But without us, the world will never be the same.

Our enemy has always been Communism. It takes any form it needs to reach its objectives. Communism has its foundation in the writings of one Karl Marx. Communism has always been the enemy of freedom and it always will. It is still alive and well and active right in our backyards.

In addition, today, we have a new enemy known as Islam. We are forbidden from calling them the enemy … but they are. What we know today as political correctness prevents honest debate and discussion in America? Political correctness is a tool of the enemy. Obamunism is not politically correct. We will look at the reality of Islam. But first, let's look at communism past and present.

Many people in America call Obama a Marxist. Communism began with Karl Marx. What is a Marxist? It is one who follows the beliefs and writings of Karl Marx. Who is Marx? Let's take a brief look at his life.

1. He was born May 5, 1818 in Treves, Germany. He came from a family of distinguished scholars and rabbi's. When he was 6 years of age his father decided to turn his back on his past. He denounced all religion and professional pursuits.

2. Marx distinguished himself in school until he went to college. He became estranged from his family when he joined a drinking club, demanding money from his family and staying drunk most of the time.

3. He studied law until his father died and then switched to philosophy. He chose as his motto a quote from Prometheus, "In one word – I hate all the gods!" He fell in with a left wing group at the University of Bonn whose single goal was to 'use their whole energy to liquidate Christianity'. The University of Bonn did not appreciate his anti-Christian views and an advisor told him to take up studies at the University of Jena. He obtained a Doctor of Philosophy there in April of 1841.

4. He married the daughter of a German Aristocrat in 1843, and together they committed to rewrite history. At the time of the wedding Marx was unemployed and would remain so his entire life. He began writing revolutionary material and was not allowed in German universities.

5. He then met Friedrich Engels, the son of a bourgeois businessman who shared his philosophies and would finance Marx for much of his life. They collaborated on what would become communist theory and wrote, "We say: A la guerre comme a la guerre; we do not promise any freedom, nor any democracy"

In 1847 Marx and Engels were invited to participate in a meeting held in Brussels by what was then known as the Communist League. The two swiftly hijacked the meeting and produced what became known as the *Manifesto to the World* and later became, the *Communist Manifesto*.

The *Communist Manifesto* as written by Marx and Engels stood for the following five principles:

1. The overthrow of Capitalism.

2. The abolition of private property.

3. The elimination of family as a social unit.

3. The overthrow of all world governments.

4. The establishment of a communist order with communal ownership of property in a classless, stateless society.

Karl Marx spent the rest of his life fomenting hatred and revolution as a way to make his philosophies work. The sad key to his personal motivation is found in his favorite quote:

*"If we can but weld our souls together,
then with contempt shall I fling my glove in the world's face,
then shall I stride through the wreckage a creator."*

Karl Marx

Marx was described as arrogant and obnoxious and only interested in provoking violent revolution. He pursued this course at the expense of his family. His wife lived in poverty, never complaining and being fed by neighbors when they could. He had a daughter die in 1852, two years later a son died and two years later a baby died at birth.

His wife wrote of her tremendous struggles, one being kicked from their home. She also wrote of supporters giving money to Marx and him spending it all and providing her no relief. At that time, he was away organizing labor unions to revolt in Italy, Germany, France, Poland and Holland.

While he never succeeded in 'his' revolutionary work, his writings led to Trotsky, Lenin and Joseph Stalin in Russia. They wreaked incredible havoc and brought the enemy called Marxism to the world for all to see. It was ugly then and it's ugly now.

So what does this have to do with President Obama? We'll put the pieces together as we go. You must think about Marx and his philosophies as we move toward today's enemy within. Stay awake and alert and you'll see the signs around you, perhaps for the first time.

Marx philosophies took root with Lenin and Stalin in Russia. They both turned out to be very bad people. They both attempted to implement the writings and philosophy of Marx. That led to the Union of Soviet Socialist Republics. In modern times it was known as the USSR, or as generally referred to, Russia. That's the reason many of us grew up under the umbrella of school air raids, hide under our desk drills and bomb shelters in our backyards.

Russia was the bad guy and their worst guy of all was Joseph Stalin. Stalin was originally born with the name of Djugashvili in 1879 in the town of Gori near the Turkish border. His mother was a baker and his father a shoemaker and also an alcoholic.

He was enrolled in a theological seminary where he quickly joined one of a number of secret societies. He was expelled from seminary for a lack of religious vocation. Once outside, Stalin spent his life as a Marxist revolutionary. He bombed his first bank in 1907. That bank would not be the end of his career as a criminal.

During the Russian Revolution against the Tsar in 1917 the five pillars of communism were nowhere to be found. Lenin was in exile in Switzerland, Trotsky was in exile in New York and Stalin was in prison in Siberia. The Russian Revolution was led by some of its finest people. They removed the Tsar and started a Provisional Government.

The new Provisional Government wanted to move toward democracy. With that in mind, they welcomed all dissidents from overseas back into the fold. It would prove to be their undoing. Lenin, Trotsky and Stalin returned.

The three immediately organized a communist uprising that failed. They went back into exile as leaders of the Bolsheviks, which means majority. The truth was the Bolsheviks weren't a majority and weren't welcome. The truth didn't stop Lenin. He operated underground and established a Red Guard to enforce his will.

An election was held in November of that year and over 75% of the voters in the Provisional Government elections voted for democracy, not communism. They knew that communism was simply socialism with the Red Guard enforcing the rules. The Bolshevik's weren't happy.

Lenin, who at that time was the leader of the Bolsheviks, then demanded that the people's congress step down and turn all power over to the Congress of Soviets, or communists. It was preposterous and illegal, but that didn't stop Lenin. The next morning following his demands, Lenin's Red Guard showed up and threatened to kill the politicians if they did not cede power to Lenin. The coup was complete. Lenin was in charge.

Lenin immediately pulled Russia from World War I in payment for Germany helping him to return to his homeland. He also began implementing his communist plan outlined earlier. He took all land from the people, took wages from the workers, closed all churches and tried as Marx had outlined, to create the ideal classless society.

By July of 1918 the people of Russia reached their boiling point. They created a White Guard to go up against the Red Guard of Lenin. He created a huge Army to control the people.

He also created a secret police who took down tens of thousands who opposed him in the Civil War. Lenin made it complete by taking out and murdering the Tsar and his family, who were residing in Russia, no longer leading the country.

During 1921 and 1922 Lenin realized his failure in following Marx when production in Russia had come to a standstill. 33 million Russians were starving and 5 million had died. He realized his adventure into Marxism was a failure. The people of the United States provided food for 10 million Russians that year and Lenin wanted it to change course.

After a civil war that cost 28 million Russian lives, Lenin introduced a program known as the New Economic Program or NEP. He returned to private land ownership and private business ownership, and the economy of Russia picked up. The cities were once again experiencing prosperity.

Unfortunately, Lenin did not live to see the success of the seeds he planted with NEP. He died in 1924 leaving a power vacuum in the leadership of the USSR. On his deathbed, Lenin wrote an appeal to the members of the Politburo, begging them not to let Stalin take over his country.

> He wrote, "*Stalin is too rude, and this fault, entirely supportable in relations among us Communists, becomes insupportable in the office of the General Secretary.*
>
> *Therefore, I propose to the comrades to find a way to remove Stalin from that position and appoint to it another man who in all respects differs from Stalin ... namely, more patient, more loyal, more polite, and more attentive to comrades, less capricious, etc.*

This circumstance may seem an insignificant trifle, but I think that from the point of view of preventing a split, and from the point of view of the relation between Stalin and Trotsky ... it is not a trifle, or it is such a trifle as may acquire decisive significance."

Our world would have been a much more peaceful and pleasant place had the Politburo heeded the dying words of Lenin. But it was not to be.

Stalin did take over and immediately ran out all significant opposition. Trotsky fled to Mexico but was eventually chased down and murdered. The Russian people were soon returned to the dreaded starvation bread made of birch bark they had known before. Stalin's rise to power proved to be Russia's last gasp for democracy.

The prosperous class of Kulak peasant's fled to the Caucasus Mountain's but it wasn't enough. Stalin knew they were resisters and ordered them wiped out in an act of genocide. They were leveled to the ground by artillery and ground troops from the military. All men, women and children, except 2,000, were murdered. The 2,000 who remained alive were shipped off to central Asia.

Stalin would go on to murder over 20 million of his own people before he died. He would claim to persuade Japan to attack America in World War II. He would see his role and that of the USSR to promote and be home to communism, which he believed must take over the world. He believed he (USSR) should sponsor revolt in every country that would accept him.

As with Marx, a quote from Stalin says it all:

"To choose one's victim, to prepare one's plans minutely, to stake an implacable vengeance and then go to bed ... there is nothing sweeter in the world."

For reasons still unclear, the United States became the first world power to recognize Stalin's Russia. The recognition took place under a Democratic President. It would prove to be a deal with the devil. The American policy of generosity was extended to the communist state in World War II in the form of what was called Lend-Lease to Russia.

The Lend-Lease program was specifically designed to provide military aid to Russia so they could fight the Germans during World War II in Europe. Congress was not comfortable with Russia, so they wrote in specific limitations to the program. They intended there to be no non-military aid of any kind given to the communist regime.

Shortly after the ink dried on Congress' limitations, the diplomatic reality came to light. General John R. Deane, head of the US Military Mission in Moscow, denied a Russian request for 25 large 200 horsepower Marine generators.

He knew the ones previously sent under the program were still sitting in crates, rusting. He knew they were being saved for post-war use. Harry Hopkins, the head of the Lend-Lease Program overruled General Deane and over the next two years 1,305 of these engines, costing over $30,000,000, were sent to Russia. Then in a more blatant move, Mr. Hopkins then ordered US orders for materials be prioritized behind that of Russia. Isn't it interesting that one of our own political appointees would do such a thing?

The program operated out of the Great Falls Air Base in Great Falls, Montana. Major George Jordan, the head of the boots on the ground in Great Falls, at the risk of his career, performed an analysis towards the end of the war. He discovered that we had sent over $3 billion in American goods of all kinds to Russia, at a time Russia was nearly bankrupt and out of business as a world power.

Major Jordan would later testify before Congress about the night he ordered Russian guards held at bay by US soldiers as he personally inspected 50 black suitcases he was ordered to allow through to Russia. What he found was suitcases filled to the brim with government documents outlining work on the Manhattan Project, our Atomic bomb in the works. They were found to be from Alger Hiss and Harry Hopkins.

He was later ordered to be quiet about a 'chemical powder' being shipped to Russia from Great Falls. When he protested, a Russian Officer called Mr. Hopkins and that was that. The shipment passed through and turned out to be Uranium. Four years after the United States exploded its first atomic bomb; Russia did so as well, years ahead of what the world believed to be possible.

US policy going forward was set by the President and his key Advisors. One of those key Advisors was none other than Harry Hopkins. When William C. Bullitt, our first US Ambassador to Russia, returned from his post in 1933, he had words for the President.

Ambassador Bullitt advised President Roosevelt that he should not trust Stalin. He shared his personal experiences and observations and warned the President about dealing with Communist leaders.

The President replied: "Bill, I don't dispute your facts; they are accurate. I don't dispute the logic of your reasoning. I just have a hunch that Stalin is not that kind of a man. Harry (Hopkins) says he is not, and that he doesn't want anything but security for his country. And I think that if I give him everything that I can, and ask nothing from him in return … he won't try to annex anything, and will work with me for a world peace and democracy." This action took place under a Democratic President.

So what does all this have to do with America today? Everything! During World War II and after, we had communist sympathizers in the White House. Many people, like legendary FBI Director J. Edgar Hoover, knew that the American Communist Party had infiltrated our highest levels of government. And the Liberal forces in America tried to silence him just like you see happening today.

So what happened with Russia? Stalin advanced into China and took Manchuria and North Korea. They also supported the founding of the Communist Chinese Army. The Chinese at that time were under the leadership of Chiang Kai-shek. They were working to create a democracy in China. They did not want the communists in China. We were their allies and agreed to support them.

Chiang decided to kick the communists out and disarm them. To everyone's surprise, we intervened on behalf of the Chinese Communists just as we had supported Russia. I find that interesting. General Marshall was installed to negotiate a truce between Chiang's democratic China and Mao's communist forces. The Chinese Communists went back on their word many times. Marshall gave up and asked to be recalled. He then became our Secretary of State.

General Wedemeyer was sent to replace Marshall. He issued a highly critical report of the peace plan Marshall was following and recommended immediate aid to Chiang Kai-shek's regime. His report went straight to the people he was criticizing and fell on deaf ears, never to be acted upon.

When push came to shove, the United States withdrew its support from democratic China, and the Chinese Communists drove Chiang and his Army into the sea. He withdrew to Formosa which is today Taiwan. Please note that Taiwan is a prosperous democracy today and one of our allies. This action took place under a Democratic President.

In 1949 it seemed obvious that Americans couldn't trust the communists. Dozens of American Communists were finally arrested by the FBI. Ex-Communist agents were coming forward in mass and spilled their guts as to the depth and width of the operation to subvert America. Yet our State Department held a meeting to discuss foreign policy going forward and shocked most in attendance with their strategy.

Here are just a few of the policies they endorsed:

- Russian Communists should not be considered as aggressive as Hitler.

- Communist China should be recognized by the United States.

- The Chinese Communist should be allowed to take over Formosa (Taiwan).

- The Chinese Communists should be allowed to take over Hong Kong from the British.

- No aid should be sent to Chiang or the anti-communist guerrillas in South China.

Two of the leaders of this conference were Lawrence Rosinger and Owen Lattimore. Both were later identified as members of the Communist Party. Do you still believe that what happened then couldn't be happening today? You must continue to read this book and be ready to take action.

The policies recommended here were not supported by the Joint Chiefs of Staff. They wanted military aid to Chiang's Chinese Nationalist Forces. However, new Secretary of State Dean Acheson announced several new policies that didn't bode well for a free China.

Acheson's announcement validated many points made in the State Department conference mentioned earlier. He also announced that the United States defense perimeter in Asia would not include Formosa or South Korea. The announcement was a signal, real or imagined that the Communists could do what they wanted.

The Yalta agreement after World War II allowed the Russians to continue to occupy Manchuria and North Korea. The Russians turned over leadership to North Korea only after installing a Communist government and building a massive army backed by the most modern equipment.

At the time, our communist within, US Diplomat Owen Lattimore said, "The thing to do is let South Korea fall, but not let it look as if we pushed it." Six months later on June 25, 1950 the North Koreans rolled into South Korea ushering in what would be the Korean War. Four years and over 54,000 American lives later, it ended where it started – at the 38th parallel. This action took place under a Democratic President.

During the war General Douglas MacArthur was the man in charge of the boots on the ground. His forces finally pushed the Chinese back; he had them on the run to the Yalu River. He had a plan to win the war.

He proposed pushing the Chinese Communists across the Yalu River with a bombing campaign on the other side of the river to stop the supplies coming from Communist China. He was loudly chastised for such a plan and told all we wanted was 'Communist Containment'. His hands were tied as the casualties mounted.

Being the great leader he was, his frustrations boiled over and he answered a letter of inquiry from Congressman Joseph Martin. He told the truth about our winning the battle and losing the war. His letter was read in Congress on December 6, 1950. A mere five days later he was relieved of command by President Truman, a Democratic President.

The Korean War, it turned out, was an extension of the same policies that left Chiang Kai-shek hanging out to dry in Formosa. All from a country committed to democracy. It makes you wonder doesn't it? It wasn't long after the war, that it was discovered that British Diplomats Donald MacLean and Guy Burgess were Russian spies. They fled behind the Iron Curtain after being discovered but not before they influenced war policy in the US and Great Britain.

America finally awakened to some real world realities under President Eisenhower. He knew that Communist appeasement was not working. He knew the United Nations did not work. To fight the Korean War only 16 nations sent a minimal amount of troops. The United States and South Korea bore the brunt of the fighting and the casualties. At the end of the war we understood for the first time the depth of infiltration in both the United States and British governments. Reality hit hard.

While they denied it, both the British and Russian governments were found to be breaking the embargo of the Chinese communists during the war. They both were supplying them in spite of the UN embargo.

Thanks to J. Edgar Hoover's persistent pursuit of the enemy here at home, many communist spies were discovered and successfully prosecuted. The FBI discovered the chain of agents responsible for stealing the secrets to the Atomic Bomb and much more. Many infiltrators were revealed and successfully prosecuted.

One of the communists' admitted failures was penetrating Hoover's FBI. Their further attempts to discredit the FBI were unsuccessful. Their goal was to portray the FBI as America's Gestapo. They admitted failure, although an element of America still believes the communist Doctrine.

The goal of communism is to build a nameless, stateless society where leadership of the party is all that matters. They believe there is no God, and therefore, superior men must rule. The precursor to communism is socialism. Their intention is to rule the world and impose their will on the masses, because they believe it to be the only way.

As Dr. Phil says, "How's that working for ya?" After the Korean War, it wasn't working very well. In 1954, Russia was producing even less food than it had in 1928. Russians were then working 38 hours to produce the same food it took just 26 hours to produce in 1928. In short, Socialism wasn't working and has never worked to this day.

Mao Tse-tung came to power in China as did Nikita Khrushchev in Russia. Many years have transpired and Mao became the largest mass murderer in the history of the world. Yet we have people in our current administration who love his philosophy.

Khrushchev became known as the Hangman of the Ukraine. He was sent there by Stalin to bring order to a people who wanted democracy. He is reported to have murdered eighty percent of them in his reign as Dictator of the Ukraine.

We are as in danger today from our enemy within as we ever were during the times outlined above. Your vote is required to drive out the enemy within. Your vote is needed today more ever before.

We don't need the change our President is trying to implement. We need the change that will save the America we know and love. I truly believe it is now, in 2012, or never.

I'll shorten the history lesson. We can take the communist thread we've been talking about and tie it to the Cuban revolution where we ended up supporting Castro, a communist, over Batista. A few years later came the Cuban Missile crises, when Kennedy stared down Khrushchev.

The thread then runs through French Indochina and eventually the Vietnam War where we lost over 58,000 American lives. We were executing the exact same strategy that cost MacArthur his career in Korea, the one influenced by the 'communists within' our country at that time.

We did not fight to win, I know, I served two years in Vietnam fighting with the Marines in and near the DMZ. We fought with rules of engagement that tied our hands just as they are tied today in Iraq and Afghanistan. Why do you think that is? There is something seriously wrong in our government and we must fix it and it must be now!

We'll now take a look at the communist goals as set in the late 60's and the bridge they built to today. Then we will look at the man and his mission, Barack Hussein Obama.

"The Communist threat from without must not blind us to the Communist threat from within. The latter is reaching into the very heart of America through its espionage agents and a cunning, defiant, and lawless communist party, which is fanatically dedicated to the Marxist cause of world enslavement and destruction of the foundations of our republic."

J. Edgar Hoover
FBI Director

"I believe that banking institutions are more dangerous to our liberties than standing armies."

Thomas Jefferson

The Announced Goals of Our Enemy

Russia and Communism were once reported on by a US Ambassador as, "The whole governmental system is the most atrociously barbarous in the world. There is on earth no parallel example of a polite society so degraded, a people so crushed, and an official system so unscrupulous."

That's plain and simple. If you still don't believe, listen to the words of one of their former leaders, born Vladimir Ilich Ulyanov, his revolutionary name in Russia was Nikolai Lenin. He was known to some as Vladimir Lenin.

He said, "Marxists have never forgotten that violence will be an inevitable accompaniment of the collapse of Capitalism ... and of the birth of the Socialist society." Lenin leaves no doubt. Think Occupy Wall Street, Greek violence in the streets and riots every time World leaders meet.

The actual Communist time table was captured in documents seized near the end of the Korean War. It was placed into the Congressional Record by Senator William Knowland in April 1954. The timetable for taking over the world was 1973. Of course that didn't happen, for many reasons. But the threat did not end. As I outline a few of the Communist goals you need to think about what is happening in this country today.

The goals were as follows:

- We have to; until we are certain of victory, take a course which will not lead to war.

- Press for all advantages but back down before war.

- Britain must be placated by being convinced that ... the Communists and the capitalist countries can live in peace. Opportunities for trade will influence the British mind.

- In the case of France, she must feel greater security in cooperating with us.

- Japan must be convinced that rearmament endangers national security. Her desire for trade will offer her great possibilities.

- The United States must be isolated by all possible means.

- In the case of India, only peaceful means should be adopted. Any employment of force will alienate us from the Arabic countries and Africa.

- After India, the Philippines and the Arab nations can be easily solved by economic cooperation.

- Then a wave of revolution will sweep Africa, and they can be driven into the sea.

Their goals lead from colonialism to capitalism to chaos to communism. The desire was to use the African/Asian stranglehold to cause the economy of Europe to collapse. They believed that the European crisis would bring a crushing economic collapse to the United States. As for Canada and South America, they will be left completely hopeless and defenseless. Keep in mind, these goals were written over five decades ago.

Let me ask a simple question. Do any of these goals ring a bell? Did Russia push and then back down in the Cuban Missile Crisis? They sure did. Did they act as the Puppet Master in the Vietnam War? What about France? They've been patsies to the Soviets for years.

India has been left alone, and they're now prospering economically. Is Europe in economic upheaval? Are many countries on the verge of bankruptcy? Does chaos describe the world today?

That brings us to America. Are we increasingly isolated? Yes. Are we facing economic collapse? Yes. But you say not from the Communists? Read on and we'll see about that one. Remember, one of their tenets is to make alliances with anyone who will get them closer to their goal of world domination. There's a new group interested in world domination we'll discuss in the chapters ahead.

Let's first look at the goals of the American Communist Party as they entered the 1960's. As you read these goals think about our world today, and the changes since these words were written. A growing number of Americans outwardly support the move to a more 'Socialist' society. Many unwittingly support the goals described here in the name of either political correctness or worse, social progress towards peace, or just plain government support.

It is important for every reader to study these points and give serious consideration to how many have actually happened:

American Communist Party Goals Circa 1960

- US acceptance of coexistence as the only alternative to atomic war.

- US willingness to capitulate in preference to engaging in atomic war.

- Develop the illusion that total disarmament by the United States would be a demonstration of moral strength.

- Permit free trade between all nations regardless of Communist affiliation and regardless of whether or not items could be used for war.

- Extension of long term loans to Russia and Soviet satellites.

- Provide American aid to all nations regardless of Communist affiliation.

- Grant recognition of Red China and its entry into the United Nations.

- Prolong conferences to ban atomic tests because the US has agreed to suspend tests as long as negotiations are in progress.

- Allow all Soviet satellites representation in the UN

- Promote the UN as the only hope for mankind. If its charter is rewritten, demand that it be set up as one-world government with its own independent armed forces.

- Do away with all loyalty oaths.

- Capture one or both of the political parties in the United States.

- Use technical decisions of the courts to weaken basic American institutions by claiming their activities violate civil rights.

- Get control of the schools. Use them as transmission belts for socialism and current Communist propaganda. Soften the curriculum. Get control of teachers' associations. Put the party line in textbooks.

- Gain control of all student newspapers.

- Use student riots to foment public protests against programs or organizations which are under Communist attack.

- Infiltrate the press. Get control of book-review assignments, editorial writing, and policy-making positions.

- Continue degrading American culture by degrading all forms of artistic expression.

- Control the critics and Directors of art museums.

- Eliminate all laws governing obscenity by calling them censorship and a violation of free speech and free press.

- Break down cultural standards of morality by promoting pornography and obscenity in books, magazines, motion pictures, radio and TV.

- Present homosexuality, degeneracy and promiscuity as normal, natural and healthy.

- Infiltrate the churches and replace revealed religion with social religion. Discredit the Bible and emphasize the need for intellectual maturity which does not need a religious crutch.

- Eliminate prayer or any phase of religious expression in the schools on the ground that it violates the principle of separation of church and state.

- Discredit the American Constitution by calling it inadequate, old-fashioned, out of step with modern needs, a hindrance to cooperation between nations on a worldwide basis.

- Discredit the American Founding Fathers. Present them as selfish aristocrats who had no concern for the common man.

- Belittle all forms of American culture and discourage the teaching of American history on the ground that it was only a minor part of the big picture.

- Support any socialist movement to give centralized control over any part of the culture – education, social agencies, welfare programs, mental health clinics.

- Eliminate the House Committee on Un-American activities.

- Discredit and eventually eliminate the FBI.

- Infiltrate and gain control of more unions.

- Infiltrate and gain control of more big business.

- Transfer all the powers of arrest from the police to social agencies. Treat all behavioral problems as psychiatric disorders which no one but psychiatrists can understand or treat.

- Dominate the psychiatric profession and use mental health laws as a means of gaining coercive control over those who oppose our goals.

- Discredit the family as an institution. Encourage promiscuity and easy divorce.

- Emphasize the need to raise children away from the negative influence of parents. Attribute prejudices, mental blocks and retarding of children to suppressive influence of parents.

- Create the impression that violence and insurrection are legitimate aspects of the American tradition; that students and special interest groups should rise up and use a united force to solve economic, political or social problems.

- Overthrow all colonial governments worldwide before they are ready for self-government.

- Internationalize the Panama Canal.

- Give the World Court jurisdiction over nations and individuals alike.

This list of goals was written before the Vietnam War and decades before the War on Terror. As you read the remaining chapters of this book keep these goals in mind. Think back over them and compare to your own observations. See what you think.

In the next chapter we'll take a look at the connection between Stalin and the Communist spies we found in our government, as well as a few events since then. We will cover the bridge spanning World War I through to today and how it all relates to our current man in the White House, Barack Hussein Obama. The implications are real, staggering and frightening.

"That experience guides my conviction that partnership between America and Islam must be based on what Islam is, not what it isn't. And I consider it part of my responsibility as President of the United States to fight against negative stereotypes of Islam wherever they appear."

President Barack Hussein Obama

"There can be no greater error than to expect, or calculate, upon real favors from nation to nation. It is an illusion which experience must cure, which a just pride ought to discard".

George Washington

The Mole, the Bridge and the President

We've taken a brief look at our communist enemies since World War I and their goals as they stated them around 1960. A lot has happened since the dark days of World War II and Korea. We experienced the fears of the Cuban Missile Crisis, the assassination of President Kennedy and then found ourselves in the Vietnam War. Since that time we've heard less of communism and more of Islam. In the late sixties Sirhan Sirhan, an Arab, assassinated Robert Kennedy.

Karl Marx compared communism to the mole, who digs deep and wide and comes up inside. Communism is the mole, the enemy of America. It got its roots in Marxism, came to fruition under Stalin and continues to this day. What I am about to share is the bridge, the bridge to Barrack Hussein Obama.

Let's begin by taking a quick look at the Cuban Missile Crisis. In regard to this event, think back to these two communist tenets:

- We have to; until we are certain of victory, take a course which will not lead to war.

- Press for all advantages but back down before war.

Interesting? To the world we were on the brink of destruction. In reality, it was a move tied directly to our enemies stated goals.

When you think of the Korean War, the Vietnam War and many little conflicts we have been involved in, remember that Stalin believed Russia should support every revolution anywhere in the world. That led to America's Domino Theory of defending the free in every revolution anywhere in the world.

During the Vietnam War there were many demonstrations on college campuses, in cities and throughout the country. While protests and demonstrations are the right of every American, I was always concerned regarding the source of the unrest. Think about these communist tenets regarding the unrest that took place in the 60's:

- Use technical decisions of the courts to weaken basic American institutions by claiming their activities violate civil rights

- Get control of the schools. Use them as transmission belts for socialism and current Communist propaganda. Soften the curriculum. Get control of teachers' associations. Put the communist party line in textbooks.

- Gain control of all student newspapers.

- Use student riots to foment public protests against programs or organizations which are under anti-Communist attack.

- Infiltrate the press. Get control of book-review assignments, editorial writing, and policy-making positions.

- Eliminate all laws governing obscenity by calling them censorship and a violation of free speech and free press.

- Eliminate the House Committee on Un-American activities.

Do you think that what happened in the United States during the 60's and 70's was just a coincidence? Do you think they were just young Americans opposing the war? Think again. Let's take a look at a few of the organizations supporting campus unrest during that time and how they have ties to the socialists and communists of old.

The four radical organizations of the 60's were the Students for a Democratic Society, The Black Panther Party, The Youth International Party (YIPPIES) and the Weather Underground. The biggest and most famous is the Students for a Democratic Society (SDS).

As we look at their evolution, we'll blend in America's attempts at stopping such activities, some of their actions and that of our government and where it brings us in the end.

We'll also take a look at Congress' attempt to control communism through the House Committee on Un-American Activities. We'll explain it step-by-step. The communist actions are in regular type. The government's actions are in bold:

- SDS of today originated first from a socialist group known as the Intercollegiate Socialist Society (ISS) which started in 1905. The ISS acted as the unofficial educational arm of the Socialist Party of America. The focus of the ISS was on students.

- **In 1918, Congress commissioned the Overman Committee to investigate German influence in the liquor industry, the growing impact of Russia after the Russian Revolution of 1917 and the Bolshevik's influence in Russia. World War I ended in 1918 and the commission was adjourned in 1919.**

- Around 1920, the Intercollegiate Socialist Society (ISS) changed its entire focus and its name to the League for Industrial Democracy (LID). The focus of LID was to spread socialism to the growing industrial world.

- In 1930, Congress commissioned what became known as the Fish Committee, named after Congressman Hamilton Fish III. Its purpose was to investigate communist activities in the United States. The Committee investigated several individuals and the American Civil Liberties Union (ACLU). The result was new powers given to the Department of Justice to keep communists out of the United States.

- Around 1933, the student wing of LID was reorganized under the name Student League for Industrial Democracy (SLID). The move was precipitated by the rise in student activism during the Great Depression.

- In 1933, retired Marine Corps Major General Smedley Butler, winner of two Medals of Honor reported a fascist plot to overthrow the government. He testified before Congress that he was approached to lead the effort and be head of the new government. The Fish Commission investigated and found the Fascist plot credible but no action was ever taken against the individuals involved.

  - In 1934, Congress commissioned the Special Committee on Un-American Activities. The committee's charge was to investigate how foreign and Nazi propaganda was getting into the United States.

The committee was chaired by John W. McCormack a Democrat from Massachusetts and Samuel Dickstein a Democrat from New York. The committee conducted massive interviews and compiled over 4,000 pages of documents during its work. A few years later it was discovered that Congressman Dickstein was in fact a Soviet spy.

- SLID in 1935 merged with the Communist National Student League to create the popular front American Student Union. During the 1930's these groups were active on college campuses fighting for free speech and student rights. They were most known for their activism regarding anti-militarism. They were also involved in the support of striking mine workers.

- In 1938, the Special Committee on Un-American Activities became the House Committee on Un-American Activities. The committee investigated people and organizations with communist ties within the United States. One of the organizations the investigation focused on was the American Youth Congress.

- In 1939, First Lady Eleanor Roosevelt supported the American Youth Congress and it became the National Youth Administration. It actually operated as part of the New Deal of President Roosevelt from 1935-1939.

- In 1939, the committee issued subpoenas to the leaders of the American Youth Congress, aka National Youth Administration. The leaders were also members of the Young Communist League. They were brought before Congress to testify.

The First Lady attended their testimony and had them stay at the White House while in Washington.

- In 1941, the American Student Union was dropped as an organization due to pressure from Congressional Investigations regarding their connections to Russia and communism.

- In 1945, the House Committee on Un-American Activities became a permanent committee in Congress.

- In 1946, the House Committee on un-American Activities investigated the infiltration of communists into the Work Progress Administration (WPA), the Federal Theater Project and the Federal Writers Project.

- In 1947, the committee investigated alleged communist propaganda in the motion picture industry. The actors and screenwriters called before Congress refused to testify and pleaded the Fifth Amendment. They were blacklisted and eventually fired from their jobs. They became known as the Hollywood Ten. In the end, they identified a total of 151 people as communists or communist sympathizers.

- Student activity remained dormant on college campuses until 1946 when the Student League for Industrial Democracy (SLID) was reborn.

- In 1948, the committee interviewed previously discovered spy, Whittaker Chambers. Chambers was a former Time Magazine Foreign Desk Editor. He detailed many people inside the federal government who were communist spies. Many of those identified were either already dead or left the country. One, Alger Hiss, pleaded not guilty but was later convicted and imprisoned.

- In 1959, former President Harry Truman denounced the House Committee on Un-American Activities as 'anything but American'.

- In 1960, SLID changed its name to the Students for a Democratic Society (SDS). One of the major players in the name and organization change was Tom Hayden, future husband of Jane Fonda. Hayden's charter was primarily accepted as the organization's new charter in what became known as the Port Huron Statement.

  SDS developed because leaders of SLID felt the phrase "industrial democracy" sounded too narrow and too labor oriented, making it more difficult to recruit students. SDS adopted what they called an anti-anti-communist stance. They also brought into the fold high profile members of the Communist Party USA.

- SDS held its first meeting in 1960 on the University of Michigan campus at Ann Arbor, Michigan.

- In 1960, the House Committee on Un-American Activities held hearings in San Francisco City Hall which led to riots by students at University of California-Berkeley.

The riots with the police led to several actions on both sides. The committee produced an anti-communist film, 'Operation Abolition' which was quickly followed by a film produced by the ACLU entitled, 'Operation Correction.' It was the beginning of the end for the House Committee on Un-American activities.

- In 1960, President Kennedy sent Advisors to Vietnam and doubled that number in 1962.

- In 1962, the SDS, led by Tom Hayden reaches agreement with LID members to permit communists into their organization.

- In 1965, the United States lands first combat troops in Vietnam.

- In 1966, the Black Panther Party for Self-Defense was founded in Oakland, California by Huey Newton and Bobby Seale. The Black Panther Party led to the creation of the Black Liberation Army. The Party's goal was to wage guerilla warfare in the United States.

From 1965 to 1975, there was much confusion in the United States due to the Civil Rights movement and the various activities of the groups noted. It was a very tumultuous time for America. The media approached the events and groups as singular, never exploring the possibility of connections with communist countries.

It is well to note here that the Students for a Democratic Society were the leaders of the majority of campus unrest during this time.

The news media treated the SDS as a youth led revolution much like what we'll read about the Arab Spring happening right now. The media treated it as purely a youth revolt.

The SDS worked with other organizations to implement sit-ins on college campuses, protests, created their own anti-war newspapers and their work eventually led to violence across America.

- In early 1968, the North Vietnamese conducted the Tet Offensive across South Vietnam.

- The American media hailed the Tet Offensive as a North Vietnamese victory and an American defeat. It is well to note that on the battlefield, the North Vietnamese were soundly defeated. In books after the war North Vietnamese General Giap admitted had the Americans counter attacked at that point, the North Vietnamese Army would have been defeated.

- It is worth noting that the American media failed to mention that during the Tet Offensive the North Vietnamese summarily executed thousands of South Vietnamese who supported Americans. In the old Imperial Capitol of Hue City, they lined up and executed in excess of 2,000 South Vietnamese who were supporting American efforts for freedom.

- The Tet Offensive, protests and media coverage resulted in President Johnson stepping aside and not running for re-election in 1968.

- In June of 1968, Robert Kennedy, brother of President Kennedy, was running for President and was assassinated. His killer was Palestinian immigrant, Sirhan Sirhan.

- In August of 1968, members of the SDS and the Yippies disrupted the Democratic National Convention in Chicago which led to brutal violence between the protestors and the police within the city.

- As a result Abby Hoffman, Jerry Rubin (Yippies) and Tom Hayden (SDS) and five others were brought to trial in Chicago on charges of conspiracy and inciting riots. They became known as the Chicago Eight.

- **In 1969, the House Committee on Un-American Activities, under pressure to stop their activities, was renamed the House Internal Security Committee.**

- In 1969, a more radical arm of the SDS emerged. The SDS was disbanded and the Weatherman or Weather Underground was established. The Weather Underground had as its founding members Bill Ayers and his wife, Bernardine Dohrn.

There was much more that happened through 1969, but far too much information to cover here. What is worth covering is the connections between the leaders of these so-called 'peace movements' and our communist enemies during the war.

Let's look at a few examples of these movements and their connections to communism.

- **Cuban Intelligence:**

In 1969, Cuban intelligence defectors identified the SDS as the organization on which they were focusing their attention. The two Cuban objectives in supporting SDS were first, to support groups that foment societal disorder, and second, create catalytic, violent acts that spawn new revolutionaries. They also sought connections with other violent US groups.

The Cuban government became quite involved with SDS as an organization. From an organizational point of view, they resurrected what was known as Venceremos Brigades, from the Che Guevara era. These were small revolutionary units used in the Cuban revolution. They wanted the SDS to use them within the US.

According to the Illinois Crime Commission over 692 Americans traveled to Cuba for training under the auspices of the Students for a Democratic Society. The Cuban government considered Operation Venceremos a huge success.

When the government closed in on some groups, their leaders were given asylum in Cuba. The most well known were Eldrige Cleaver and Robert Franklin Williams.

As late as 2003 there were still 74 fugitives from this era being housed by the Cubans? At the time, most fugitives were entering Cuba via Canada. Stokely Carmichael is another who visited and trained there and openly worked with Cuban Intelligence.

Huey Newton fled to Cuba with his wife to avoid trial for murder, embezzlement and assault charges. They were treated well and given an apartment and jobs. Newton would eventually become disenchanted and return to the United States because the Cubans made him work while there. His return to the US was not welcomed by party leaders. Newton would continue to lead a life of crime and was eventually murdered in the streets of Oakland, California.

- **Chinese Communists:**

In 1968, a US citizen by the name of Liebel Bergman returned to the United States after two years in Communist China. He founded an organization known simply as, RU.

The mission of RU was stated as, 'We recognize the need for armed struggle against the power of the state and assume responsibilities of revolutionaries in the preparation of that struggle'.

He sought the help of dissident groups in the United States including the Black Panther Party and the SDS. They sought to use the war in Vietnam as the fuel for their revolutionary fire.

Bergman later spent a week in Paris where he met with Chinese agents. He was also successful in getting his daughter-in-law into a prominent SDS position where she was used to personally select key members for the revolutionary Cuban Venceremos Brigades. Members of RU were behind the 1971 violent riots in San Jose when President Nixon was visiting the city.

Black Panther, Robert Franklin Williams, went from Cuba to China. The Chinese communists welcomed him with open arms. He was treated as royalty, given a luxury apartment and chauffeured limousine. They used him for propaganda purposes and willingly let him return to the States in 1969.

Williams returned and testified before Congress and his previous kidnapping charges were later dropped. Williams received a Ford Fellowship to teach at the University of Michigan.

The CIA infiltrated the organization effectively and discovered their real intent and purpose. The two agents testified before Congress of the threat and level of funding being provided by the Chinese. Congress listened. Less than nine months later they brought CIA Director Richard Helms before them to be chastised for his actions of infiltrating the organization.

- **Russian Communists**:

The Russian communists had been active in the US during the 30's, 40's and 50's as we'll discuss later in this book. They provided financial support to the Communist Party USA up to and until the dissolution of the USSR in the late 80's.

During World War II, Communist Party USA was active in recruiting over 400 Americans to get involved in espionage for the Russians. When the fall of the Berlin Wall occurred funding from Russia dried up.

- **The Weather Underground:**

The Weather Underground (WU) emerged from an SDS meeting in Chicago in 1969. In attendance were representatives of the Communist Party USA, the Progressive Labor Party, the Socialist Workers Party, the Radical Youth Movement (RYM) and the Yippies to mention a few.

Out of that meeting emerged a group committed to the violent overthrow of America. The RYM group would morph into what became known as the Weather Underground. It is well to note that two of the key leaders of this group are Bill Ayers and Bernardine Dohrn, his wife.

Ayers and Dohrn are the same folks who hosted the initial kickoff meeting in their home for Barack Hussein Obama when he first ran for the Illinois Senate.

The manifesto that soon came forth from the leaders of what then became known as the WUO, or Weather Underground Organization, was based on the principles of Mao Tse tung. It was also revealed, in later Senate testimony that a Cuban Intelligence Officer was the control operative that the leader of the WUO reported to.

Ayers and Dohrn advocated the aggressive and violent overthrow of the US economic system as a way to destroy the economy and the military-industrial complex. Everyone agreed but wanted the Weather Underground Organization to lead the charge. Ayers and Dohrn wanted the black liberation movement to do the dirty work.

On July 4 through the 7, 1969, several new SDS members traveled to Cuba for a meeting with the North Vietnamese. Bernardine Dohrn was in that group. The Vietnamese said they did not want the 'old' American radical they had been dealing with. They were clear that they wanted 'a more aggressive' American activist. The Vietnamese told the group of American activists it was imperative for them to act to achieve a 'political' victory in the United States if they desired the support of the Vietnamese.

The Vietnamese added that they wanted an active, guerilla war within the US. Dohrn and her cohorts returned to the US via Canada in August of 1969. Dohrn and her WUO supporters took the challenge to heart, and committed to support the Cubans and North Vietnamese.

They planned a massive demonstration in Chicago on the two year anniversary of the death of Cuban Revolutionary, Che Guevara. They executed their plan in October of 1969, and it coincided with the trial of the Chicago 8. The demonstration evolved into what became known as The Days of Rage. The demonstrators destroyed the Chicago Loop.

The news media covered the action not as something subversive, rather as 'police violence' and part of the continuing youth revolution against the war. They seemed unable to pick up on the communist ties and motivations, although many other groups did.

Soon after the Chicago destruction, Ayers, Dohrn and Jeff Jones wrote a letter for the Weather Underground paper calling for 'a revolutionary communist party to lead the struggle, to give coherence and direction to the fight, to seize power and build a new society'. Please note that two of the three are friends of our new President today.

The group was responsible for a dozen bombings against Federal property from 1970 to 1974. Those bombings were in the US Senate, New York City Police buildings and the Pentagon among others. They caused $10 million in damages and killed at least one person.

In 2001, Bill Ayers, now a Professor at the University of Chicago, wrote a book entitled *Fugitive Days: A Memoir* where he says he wanted to show that a homegrown guerilla movement was afoot in America. He earlier said, "I don't regret setting bombs. I feel we didn't do enough". When the FBI raided one of their Chicago hideouts they found what was described as enough explosives to blow up a city block.

They also found leaflets and propaganda that described their mission as being 'a guerilla organization staffed with communist men and women'. It further said their goal was 'to disrupt the United States, to incapacitate it and to attack it from the inside'. Make a mental note, or even better highlight this section right now.

As you read to the end of this book, think about these goals, and Ayers, Dohrn and our President.
Bernardine Dohrn was partners in crime with Kathy Boudin. Dohrn studied Russian at Bryn Mawr College.

Her senior year she studied at the University of Moscow. She also spent time living in Leningrad. Kathy Boudin was implicated in the Greenwich Village bombing that killed three members of the WUO. The FBI found 57 sticks of dynamite in the apartment, along with SDS pamphlets and various stolen ID's and passports.

Boudin's father, a US citizen living in the United States, was a member of the communist party and had registered with the US government as a Cuban Agent. Boudin was summoned by the Soviets, who contacted her through her father, and she was seen entering the Russian Embassy.

It was later found that the Cuban consul in Canada gave money to Boudin and another woman implicated in the bombing, Cathy Wilkerson — the money was to get them Cuba. The money made its way to the women's families via a Kuwaiti diplomatic pouch, which went to Canada and ended up with the women.

Boudin, Wilkerson and Tom Hayden (SDS) met with North Vietnamese officials in Hanoi on more than one occasion. Hayden would meet and marry Jane Fonda and they together travelled to Hanoi. On one of these visits Hanoi Jane posed for her famous picture with a North Vietnamese anti-aircraft crew.

In 1969, twenty members of the SDS traveled to Cuba to study revolution with Cuban and North Vietnamese revolutionaries. But the Weather Underground didn't stop with ties to just communists.

They began contact with Al Fatah, a Palestinian terrorist organization founded by Yasser Arafat, and the Popular Front for the Liberation of Palestine (PFLP). Both groups were part of the Palestinian Liberation Organization (PLO).

Bill Ayers even traveled to Canada to visit with the Quebec Liberation Front and returned with $2,000.00 he didn't have when he left. I'm not sure the Indian casinos were in existence at the time. Where did Ayers get his money?

The 60's and early 70's were a time of massive change and chaos in US society. The government that once had its eye on communism was beginning to look away.

- In 1972, the massacre of Israeli athletes took place at the Summer Olympics, introducing a new arm of an old enemy. It was carried out by a group calling themselves Black September.

With the Vietnam War coming to an end, protests and attacks on our government subsiding, the rise of Muslim terrorism was officially introduced to the world. It was ugly and televised live for the first time.

So what is the connection between the communist groups working to destroy America and the Muslims? Let's see what was going on around this time between the two.

During this period of time, there is no known active support of anti-war activities by the Arab Fedayeen organizations such as noted above. However, the connection comes from the Organization of Arab Students (OAS), the Foreign Students Association (FSA) and the Muslim Student Organization (MSO).

These organizations began to become active on college campuses to build support for the Palestinians against Israel. They appealed to the plight of the Vietnamese people and found fertile ground for followers on Americans campuses.

It was also at this time that the Arab States such as Saudi Arabia began bestowing large gifts to US universities who were all too happy to take their money. Ivy League universities especially received grants to start Middle Eastern Studies programs and departments. Pro-Islam Professors were endowed and the brainwashing of our students began.

The early efforts of the Fedayeen movement centered more on fund raising than military action. In the early 70's there was discussion regarding attacking American interests but no action took place at that time.

The Organization of Arab Students was the most active. They were directly tied to raising funds for Al Fatah. They had over a hundred chapters on campuses across the US. They held fund raisers and promoted Fedayeen speakers and were growing more successful by the day.

University of Texas grad student, Dr. Alami, returned to Lebanon and was a Professor at the American University there. He was also head of Al Fatah in Lebanon.

He returned to the states in 1968 to Columbia University where the OAS had created what was known as the Fundraising Committee for Palestine. It was created for the sole purpose of funneling money to Al Fatah.

The Organization of Arab Students (OAS) then traveled to Jordan to discuss their lack of support and harassment of Al Fatah. They sought their support in the terrorist activities of the Al Fatah organization. In 1969 another successful fundraiser was held at New York University.

During this time, Al Fatah was giving way to the Palestinian Liberation Organization as the leader of trouble in the Middle East. The PLO became a terrorist force that evolved into many groups at work in the world today.

- **In 1975, the House Internal Security Committee was abolished. (Formerly the House Committee on Un-American Activities)**

The Palestinian Solidarity Committee held its first meeting in New York City, January 20, 1976. The meeting was held under tight security and was attended by none other than Tom Hayden (SDS) and Liebel Bergman who had returned from China. The goal was to raise the level of attention for Arabs in the US and appeal to the more radical elements.

Yasser Arafat emerged as the leader and mouthpiece for the Arab movement. He had the support of activists and students in the United States. While he promoted himself as a poor, bedraggled Palestinian, he was in fact a killer.

Communications intercepted as early as 1973 tied Arafat to Black September terrorists. The day after the intercepts took place, the Saudi Arabian Embassy in the Sudan was seized. They took captive the US Ambassador, Cleo Noel, his assistant, George Curtis Moore, and others. Under direct orders from Arafat, Noel and Moore were both machine gunned to death the next day.

In spite of his despicable behavior, Arafat was invited to the White House in 1973. He became friends of Jimmy Carter, and later, under the Clinton Administration, he was a regular in the Oval Office. The Israeli military confined Arafat to his compound for several months. That is where he died at the age of 75. Prior to his death, groups like Hamas had already dethroned him in a quest to destroy Israel.

What we do know from merging our student organizations with those of the Arabs, and the ties with our radical 60's organizations, is that there was a beginning to today's ties with communism and Islam. It started with Arafat in the sixties and continues to this day.

Given this trail of communism and the rise of Islam, what does that mean for our current President Barack Hussein Obama? If we look at Obama's own books, he describes his 'attending socialist conferences'. He even admits to 'coming in contact with Marxist literature'. I can't help but wonder if that means he picked up the Marxist literature once – but didn't inhale? Or … well, it makes you wonder?

In one of his books he refers to a great Mentor by the name of Frank. His mentor was found to be Frank Marshall Davis.

Obama lived in Hawaii from 1971-79, and it was during this time he developed a relationship he described as 'close as a son'. He says he sought advice on his career and listened to his poetry.

Mr. Davis was well known to authorities. He is a member of the Communist Party USA. He was investigated at one time by the House Committee on Un-American Activities where he was accused of involvement with several subversive groups. Davis, in his writings, said he is big on the 'class struggle'.

He advised Obama before he left for Occidental College and is reportedly the one who pointed him to a life in Chicago. Once in Chicago, Obama was quickly brought in to the inner circle of political favor.

It was in Chicago that he connected with Bill Ayers of SDS and Weather Underground fame, and one of his former companions in crime, Carl Davidson. Davidson is currently a prominent figure in the Committee of Correspondence for Democracy and Socialism. That organization is an off shoot of the Communist Party USA.

The Mole is communism, now an unholy partner with Islam. The Bridge is what you have just read. It is naïve to think when the House Committee on Un-American Activities disappeared, so did the communist threat.

When the committee was disbanded in 1975, the CIA was immediately given a new mission. Their new mission was to begin to track terrorism and terrorist groups. They were frustrated at every turn by our bureaucracy. It was at this time in the late 60's and early 70's, that political correctness came into being.

There are two other people worth mentioning in the connection between past and present. The first is a man from the past by the name of Saul Alinsky. The second is a man of the future, George Soros.

We'll first look at Saul Alinsky. While he is mentioned elsewhere in the book, it is worth pointing out the connection of this early revolutionary with Barack Obama. Alinsky was born in Chicago and attended the University of Chicago.

He was taken by the work of community organizing and pioneered methods used by many today. Alinsky taught that, "True revolutionaries do not flaunt their radicalism. They cut their hair, put on suits and infiltrate the system from within." Alinsky taught that revolution was a slow, patient process. The trick was to penetrate existing institutions such as churches, unions and political parties. Alinsky counseled to do and say whatever it takes to gain power.

Alinsky wrote several books before his passing, the most well known was *Rules for Radicals*. He dedicated the book with these words, "Lest we forget at least an over-the-shoulder acknowledgment to the very first radical: from all our legends, mythology, and history... the first radical known to man who rebelled against the establishment and did it so effectively that he at least won his own kingdom — **Lucifer**."

Alinsky also started a training program known as the Alinsky Method. He taught his method to many people including Hillary Clinton and Barack Obama. Barack Obama for many years was a trainer for the Alinsky Method. His training was part of his 'community organizing'.

Alinsky taught what he called 'general concepts of change' to move us toward 'a science of revolution'. What he called 'change' meant massive change in our socioeconomic structure, and what he called 'organizing' meant pursuing confrontational political tactics.

Alinsky taught his followers that the Have-Nots must 'hate the establishment of the Haves' because they have 'power, money, food, security and luxury'. He claimed that 'justice, morality, law, and order, are mere words used by the Haves to justify and secure their status quo'.

Does any of that sound familiar? Do you see these actions with Obama before and after the election? Do you see them in his actions since he became President? You sure do. He represents **the enemy within**. He is their spokesperson, the man chosen to lead the final charge.

Alinsky represents the past connection of socialist, communist influence in Obama's life. George Soros is the connection to the future. Soros is one of the wealthiest men on the planet. His personal fortune of at least $7 billion and additional investments of another $11 billion allow him broad access to whatever he chooses.

He has a group of pro-Left foundations that distributes more than $400 million a year to causes ranging from underwriting left-leaning Democrat Party candidates to legalizing marijuana to advocating for euthanasia.

Soros does much of his work through his foundation known as the Open Society Institute (OPI). He is a big proponent of a one world government. The OPI funds many, many organizations in strategic areas around the world. He uses his philanthropy to drive change in the direction he desires.

Soros organizations and influence spreads far and wide and cannot be covered adequately here. What I can say is that he was a major reason for Obama's rapid rise to power. He reportedly spent $25 million of his own money attempting to get Bush out of office in 2004. He supported John Kerry and learned from his mistakes.

In June 2004 Soros hosted a fund raiser in his New York home for then Senate candidate Barack Obama. In August of 2004 Obama wows the crowd at the Democratic National Convention and springs on the national scene.

In December 2006, when Obama was contemplating a run for the White House, George Soros and Barack Obama met to discuss the young Senator's political ambitions. A few short weeks later, in January 2007 Obama announced his 'exploratory committee'. He was running for President although he had just 143 days in the US Senate.

Within hours of his announcement, Soros sent Obama the maximum individual contribution of money permitted under campaign finance law. A week later Soros announced he'd be supporting the candidacy of Barack Obama instead of Hillary Clinton, the candidate he'd previously supported.

Soros was interviewed in May, 2008. He was quite enthusiastic on Obama saying, "Obama has the charisma and the vision to radically reorient America in the world, this emphasis on experience is way overdone."

In any discussion of Barack Obama we must include Saul Alinsky and George Soros if we are to understand the man who is now our President.

Let's take a look.

"Why has Obama, for over 2 years,
employed numerous private and government attorneys
to avoid presenting a legitimate birth certificate
and college records?"

Donald Trump

"The constitution vests the power of declaring war in Congress; therefore no offensive expedition of importance can be undertaken until after they shall have deliberated upon the subject and authorized such a measure."

George Washington

Where Did Obama Come From?

I like to read Mychal Massie's columns. He is black you know, so I hope this isn't racist. In a recent column entitled, *Nero in the White House*, Mychal said, "Three significant historical events have been eclipsed by Obama: 1) Jimmy Carter will no longer be looked at as the worst president in American history; 2) Richard Nixon and Bill Clinton will no longer be recognized as the greatest liars in presidential history; 3) Clinton's stain on Monica's dress, and what that did to the White House in general and the office of the president specifically, will forever pale in comparison to the stain and stench of Obama."

Strong words, alright, about a man elected President, who the nation knows very, very little about. Okay, we know he was born in Honolulu. In the interest of full disclosure, I was born in Dover, Ohio. I actually have a birth certificate to prove it. It wouldn't take me two years and Donald Trump to produce it either.

The President produced his right away, well, no, we all know it was really after The Donald, as in Trump, was about to roast him like the chicken he is. He found that birth certificate with the wave of his magic wand. It was suddenly available. Do you ever wonder why he didn't produce it earlier, like when McCain did?

In America we always know a lot about our politicians. The media works overtime to dig up dirt. We knew about John Kennedy's back brace. We knew poor Betty Ford was an alcoholic, and that she eventually turned that to something good. She seemed like such a nice lady. We knew about Jimmy Carter's brother, who generally had a few too many beers, and that Jimmy still stuck with him.

We knew about Bill and Monica, Cheney's heart problems, the Kennedy kids and their problems and who could forget Ted Kennedy's escapades at Chappaquiddick? We knew Truman didn't go to college. We knew Bush the Younger dodged the draft but we know nothing about Obama.

Why do you suppose we don't know jack about our main man, Barack Hussein Obama? We barely know why he changed his name from Barry! Or why he visited Pakistan for a few weeks as an Occidental College student? We don't even know what Passport he used to go there? Isn't that interesting? The media found dirt on Joe the Plumber in 24 hours but nothing on Obama?

When it came to George the Younger the media was downright mean, and fast too. Before you can say "Arab Spring", the media was giving us copies of George's flight records, his college transcripts and talked to dozens of folks who partied with the then President of the United States. What's frightening is how the same media is brain dead when it comes to Obama.

We elect this guy and the media has zero interest in his background. It's troubling when you consider nothing is sacred today, except when it comes to Obama. When it came to Sarah Palin the gloves were off. Why do you suppose they pander to the imposter?

He flies onto the political scene, and strangely, the media is not the least bit interested in digging into flight path to getting here. They can find every party George the Younger ever attended, as well as his grades in every class, but nothing on Obama. They can find dirt on Herman Cain but not Obama. Wiki Leaks, the online organization dedicated to leaking government secrets, proved that our U.S. government records aren't as bullet proof as Obama's past.

It hardly seems right to me. Let's consider some facts it would be fun to know. Let's pretend we're on David Letterman's Show and this is tonight's Top Ten List:

1. How did Obama rise in politics so fast?

2. Who did he play with as a kid?

3. Why does he deny being friends with Bill Ayers and his lovely wife Bernardine Dohrn?

4. How did he and Michelle meet? What was their wedding like? Who was best man?

5. Who are the people from his past? Classmates, friends and enemies?

6. How about his years at Occidental, Columbia and Harvard? Classes, grades and friends? How did he finance college since he came from such a poor background as a child?

7. What about his law career in Chicago and his amazing rise to power having really never tried a case? And maybe releasing those records the Chicago Law School's been holding back.

8. It would be great to know how he compares his roots in Indonesia at the Madrasah to his twenty plus years listening to the Reverend Wright?

9. We'd certainly like to know if he is a closet Muslim.

---

10. I saved the best for last. I'd love the President and First Lady to sit down with Greta on Fox and explain directly two things that could help turn around our Nation's economic problems.

I'd like to know how Michelle got such a giant raise, tripling her salary as Head of Diversity, when her husband became a U.S. Senator. That would make an inspirational book. After 30 years in business, I don't know how to do that!

The second one is how did the two of them buy a big house so cheap and sell it for over a million dollars in short order? These things just don't happen. Of course on that one we'd have to k now more about his relationship with his buddy, Tony Rezko, the one who sold it to them. He's in jail now. We could all learn from our President, but he never shares his entrepreneurial genius or admits to how his connections may have helped.

What we do know about our current President pales in comparison to what we don't know. We do know a few things about his days in Chicago. He loves the Teamsters. They're headquartered there.

In an editorial by Michelle Malkin on September 9, 2011, she notes, "The 1.4 million members Teamsters Union lifted Obama to power with a coveted endorsement and bottomless campaign coffers funded by coerced member dues." Those are powerful statements. She continues, "Over the past two decades the union has donated nearly $25 million to the Democrats compared to $1.8 million for the Republicans." That gives us a clue about where he came from, eh?

And we couldn't forget his partnership with Richard Trumka, President of the AFL-CIO. He is former President of the United Mine Workers Union. That is where he earned his stripes as an organizer and strike leader.

When he was elected as President, the Communist Party USA was thrilled according to CPUSA Labor Commission Chairman, Scott Marshall, who emphasized their working relationship with AFL-CIO President Richard Trumka. Mr Marshall described their relationship as continuing efforts of 'independent' union organizations operating in, or for political campaigns in various cities.

I'm not saying Mr. Trumka is a communist. We just have to continue to remember we become who we spend our time around. One fact, well reported, is Mr. Trumka bragging about his access to the President and being in the White House at least once a week. Makes you wonder, that's for sure.

We do know that the President once taught the Alinsky Method of organizing while he was a Chicago lawyer. We also know Saul Alinsky preached partnerships with unions as part of his organizing methods. We also know that Saul Alinsky bridges the Marxist movement from World War II times into the 60's. To take a line from our President's actions ... that's all you need to know.

- Does any of this bother you?

If not, call your Doctor and have your pulse checked, you may be dead? If you're alive you may be a Liberal, or you're a participant on Jay Leno's Jaywalking segment.

Whatever the case, please read on and see what Mr. Obama did when he became our President.

"My job to the Muslim world is to communicate that the Americans are not your enemy. We sometimes make mistakes. We have not been perfect."

President Barack Hussein Obama
Apology to the Muslim world: Interview with Al Arabiya, January 27, 2009. He was inaugurated on January 20, 2009.

Our New President
Barack Hussein Obama

It was no surprise to anyone when Obama pulled off a big win. The media slobbered all over him; he raised mega-millions from what remain questionable overseas sources, and he speaks well with a teleprompter. Everyone would also agree that he had serious support from a yet unidentified group to derail the Clinton's plans for the White House.

If you're looking for all the footnotes and professorial BS in this book, you're not going to find it. I'm just going to talk to you as if we're sitting across the table having a discussion. I figure as a citizen in this great nation, a veteran and a taxpayer I shouldn't have to share my key information if the President won't share his. So let's start by looking at a few concerns we find in his story. These issues made me scratch my head.

- **The Black Issue**:

    When I would discuss the Obama issue with people, how I was struggling to support candidate Obama, a high percentage jumped on the race card. "You just don't like him because he's black", was a common and quick retort.

    First, I'd have voted for Colin Powell, I love Congressman West from Florida and find Herman Cain interesting. Second, Obama didn't grow up black in America like Martin Luther King or Thurgood Marshall or Colin Powell. If anyone uses the race card, Obama does. I also think much of Black America voted for him because he was black.

Besides, when he was in Montana he was adopted as a Crow Indian. On a trip to Ireland he agreed with a bloke over there that he was part Irish. The fact is he uses the race card and many other cards strategically, usually in response to criticism which he doesn't care much for.

- **The Reverend, Mr. Wright:**

I don't know about you, but personally, what church a person attends is his own business. I was once an Atheist and some years back became a Christian and accepted Jesus Christ. A friend many years ago put his arm around me and said, "Eddie, we can never let our differences get in the way of the fact we love each other". He was right.

 As for politicians, I just want them to have a religion that is in line with our American values. What bothers me about our President? For over twenty years, he and his wife were supposedly Christians, God fearing Americans. Then, while running for President – he lost it all and denounced his Preacher.

How could the President and his wife lose two decades of commitment and knowledge in less time than an Infomercial? Obama was dedicated to the Reverend Wright and his teachings. He took his family to church every Sunday and that's cool! But at the first hint of controversy, candidate Obama turned and ran. He tossed his Reverend under the proverbial bus.

Let's look at the problem another way. As we head into the 2012 Presidential Race, Mitt Romney and Jon Huntsman are both candidates on the Republican side. Both are devoted to the Mormon religion. Let's say the media starts making an issue of their Mormon religion. As the controversy heats up, they denounce Mormonism and walk away. They go on TV claiming to have never believed a thing they heard preached. Let me ask one simple question:

- Would that bother you?

It should! Yet Obama got a pass from the media. The same media that jumped all over Bush the Younger and would jump on it if Romney or Huntsman had done the same thing. In the least, his change of heart is a character issue. It is also an issue of integrity. A red flag popped up as my instincts went crazy over this issue. How about you?

- Does it bother you?

Now let's look at the teachings he says he ignored and didn't believe.

- **The Reverend, Mr. Wright and his Teachings:**

  When I woke up today, we still had religious freedom in America. People like the Reverend Wright can preach what they will. Just like we tolerate the nut cases in Kansas who protest military funerals, or the rattlesnake handlers--we as Americans have religious tolerance. And that is a good thing. The President can even go there if he wants, who cares?

The problem came when the world found out what the teachings of Reverend Wright really were. Mr. Obama sat for twenty years and listened to the Reverend Wright's sermons on violence, anti-white, racism, anti-Americanism, and revolution. Yet, according to him, he and Michelle didn't believe a single word of it.

The issue I am bringing to your attention has nothing to do with the particular viewpoint of the Right Reverend, although it concerns me that anyone would use a church to preach hate and revolution. The news media has missed the point, intentionally or otherwise. The real issue is what does Obama's actions really mean. To me, they mean he is either a liar, stupid or has a hidden agenda.

You cannot sit in front of a man and listen to his vitriolic ranting for two decades and not retain a great deal. To sit there with your family all those years means you must also agree with him. He is either lying about not believing these things, or, he is stupid enough to sit there and not retain anything. I haven't seen any evidence of that yet.

Lastly, he just might in fact believe these things and is privately working toward what his Mentor preaches about America. Personally, I believe, based on my observation and research, the latter. Think about it?

We're not dealing with a stupid man, he just may be brilliant. He is certainly cunning. Think back on what you read in the last two chapters and think of these actions by Obama.

- Does this bother you?

- What could his intent be?

When a man stands before you and denies his core beliefs, what does that say about his character? What could be his intent? Let's take a look at his wife Michelle and her comments when becoming our First Lady.

- **Michelle's Proudest Moment!**

    Who can forget when the new first lady, America's very first, black First Lady, proudly proclaimed her now famous quote, "I am now proud to be an American!" That certainly was a moment I'll never forget. Our new President's wife has never in her life been proud to be an American until her husband becomes President.

    Her words speak volumes about how she really feels and who she really is. I don't even doubt that she feels that way. Here is a woman who got into Princeton University because of Affirmative Action, not her grades. The America that allowed that to happen must have been okay? Maybe it's those years in Reverend Wright's church that hooked her optical nerve to her bowels.

    It is a telling statement of her bad attitude and core beliefs, America is a bad place. That bothers me, and I sure hope it bothers you, too. She's now the First Lady of the greatest nation on earth ... but not in her mind.

- Does this bother you?

- What could her intent be?

After Michelle's proudest moment, then came our new President's Apology Tour.

- **Apologies to the World for America's Terrible Behavior and the Nobel Peace Prize:**

  Do you think Barack's forgetting his Reverends teachings and his wife's rejection of America are a coincidence? Think again? Yet soon comes coincidence three, he receives the Nobel Peace Prize. He receives it having done, well, uh, nothing. No noteworthy achievements, no peacemaking and no scientific breakthroughs. That is, nothing except travel around the world apologizing for America's past behavior. I guess this could be some of the change he was talking about during the Campaign.

  Being a bit of a patriot I tried hard to figure out exactly what it was he was apologizing for. Could it be saving most of Europe during World War I? Or maybe it was saving Europe and the rest of the free world in World War II? No, maybe it was sticking around Japan after the war and rebuilding them, and coaching them into becoming one of the world's great financial powers and a wonderful people?

  I still kept wondering what he was apologizing for. Maybe it's because of the billions in aid we send both as a government and a people to countries around the world, even our enemies, when disaster strikes.

Is that what he is apologizing for? Maybe it was President Kennedy staring down the Russians during the Cuban Missile Crisis? No, what then? Maybe it was Vietnam where we were guilty of trying to help free South Vietnam from the Communist North's desire to conquer them? Or was it our enduring the 'change' taking place in America in the 60's without collapsing. Maybe that was it?

Think about it. We did not occupy one single country in any of these wars. When we conquered Japan in World War II we spent money and time rebuilding what we tore down. Look at Japan today. What is there to apologize for? But our President tried to apologize to today's Emperor.

Maybe it was George the Older who in a few days freed Kuwait from Saddam Hussein and gave it back to Kuwaiti's? Could it be our technology that leads the world in almost every category? Maybe it was our manufacturing and financial leadership that has led the world until, well, very recent times.

Maybe we shouldn't have been so aggressive, so capitalistic in our approach? I couldn't figure his bent for apologizing to anyone and everyone for being part of the greatest country the world has ever seen.

Then, over time, the thought hit me. His core beliefs were coming out in his actions. We were squared off against two Muslim countries who he likes and we weren't the America he and his wife wanted.

But he was now our President and apologize he did. And throughout the world, with the exception of our long time allies, the world ate it up.

He pushed on full speed ahead. He apologized to anyone who would give him a venue. And what did it get him? He received a very clear message from the one world government movement that he had done good. His message came in the form of the Nobel Peace Prize.

The free world was shocked. But he and his fellow Marxists were happy as kids in a candy store. Our new President, the man who wrote two Autobiographies before he'd done anything in his life, was awarded the Nobel Peace Prize. It remains one of the world's great mysteries. That is unless you think about the two preceding chapters.

- Does it bother you that he apologizes for America?

- Does it bother you that he received the Nobel Peace Prize for nothing?

One of the best quotes on the subject comes from former Congressman Newt Gingrich when he said, "As an American I am not so shocked he was given the Nobel Peace Prize without any accomplishments to his name, because America gave him the White House based on the same credentials." Think about that one.

Let's look at a little more message sending behavior – even as our troops are at war.

- **The Commander in Chief Skips the Inaugural Ball for Medal of Honor Recipients:**

  Since its inception in 1953, every President has found time to stop by the Salute to Heroes Ball during the Inauguration. Every one that is, except our new President Barrack Hussein Obama. He was too busy.

  The administration offered many reasons for his absence, like too many Inaugural Balls, but the fact is he snubbed his military.

  There are no truer heroes of our freedom than winners of the Congressional Medal of Honor. These are the special warriors of our nation. The Ball is to honor those living and dead. Our new President cannot make time for these special men.

  To me, his actions are unforgivable. At a time we have troops at war in two countries; his actions prove where his heart is regarding our nation's military. And, it's a damned shame.

  - Does this bother you?

  - Why do you think he really skipped the Medal of Honor Ball?

Think about his actions outlined in this chapter. Think about them in the context of the previous two chapters. We'll now take a look at the Presidents new staff.

*"A Marxist begins with his prime truth that all evils
are caused by the exploitation of the proletariat
by the capitalists. From this he logically proceeds
to the revolution to end capitalism, then into the third stage
of reorganization into a new social order of the dictatorship
of the proletariat, and finally the last stage -- the political
paradise of communism."*

Saul Alinsky
(Taken from *Rules for Revolutionaries* by Saul Alinsky,
Page 10. Please note this is from the course Obama
taught to other activists and community organizers
as a lawyer in Chicago.)

Obama and His Band of Socialists

I didn't start out thinking this guy was evil. I originally thought he was really, as in really, inexperienced at anything other than reading a teleprompter. He came into office with less than a weak resume. He was a do nothing Senator at the State and Federal level, always voting 'present', never committing himself.

When I listened to him speak I found him to be a great orator. He could deliver a dynamite speech as long as he was reading it from a teleprompter. But his speeches lacked any substance. In the beginning, I wished he were for real. But I continually found his words empty. I struggled, always looking for the real man.

Being President of the greatest nation on earth, the leader of the free world, requires leadership. He has none. If you think about it, where would he learn leadership? He's never held a real job, and everything has been handed to him.

I spent thirty years in Corporate America with three of the Nation's leading companies in Frito Lay, Pepsi Cola and Compaq Computer. I ended my corporate career as a Vice President of Compaq. I did that with no college, just a Marine Corps education and a lot of work. If I've seen one great talker with no substance I've seen a hundred. It was clear, when I saw Obama speak; he was just another empty suit on the way to the top.

After more than two years of his so called leadership, the debate is over. Real leadership means you have stood up, taken responsibility and delivered the desired result. You have to have more than position power if you're leader. When did he ever manage a budget? When did he ever lead more than a handful of people as a community organizer? And we're all still trying to figure out what that really means.

Yet the community organizer thing may just be quite important. That is exactly where Karl Marx started. He was out in the streets preaching his brand of socialism. After all, he didn't work; he relied on others for his support.

Like it or not, our new Sheriff, Barrack Hussein Obama rode into town and started appointing interesting people with no experience, just like himself. What made it even more interesting; in many cases he bypassed Congress by appointing what are called Czars. It was an interesting choice of words if nothing else. His first choice was our new Treasury Secretary.

- **Let Me Introduce My New Head of the Treasury, Mr. Timothy Geithner:**

  Let's be short and sweet. We introduce a guy to take care of our money and he hasn't paid his taxes to the IRS. He said he didn't know how to use Turbo Tax. There are very few Americans who don't know how to use Turbo Tax. As Willy Nelson sings, "That shit ain't right".

- Does that bother you?

The Czars are coming.

- **Czars in America: A New Way to get Your Appointment without Congressional Approval.**

  When Candidate Obama was running for President, one of the pillars of his platform was transparency. He spoke often about transparency in his planned administration and honesty and bipartisanship. What he said was all good stuff.

In a March 31, 2008 speech on the campaign trail, then Candidate Obama said, "The biggest problems that we're facing right now have to do with George Bush trying to bring more power into the executive branch and not go through Congress at all. And that's what I intend to reverse when I'm president of the United States".

That was pretty clear. Hooray for Candidate Obama. Wait a minute. Bypassing Congress with new and questionable appointments is not exactly in keeping with his statement above. Yet appoint he did.

As we review these new appointments, consider why a President would do that and the cost of doing so. We'll talk about that after checking out the positions and appointments.

- **Counselor to the Secretary of the Treasury or Car Czar:**

  Let's start with a Counselor to Stephen Geithner. His name is Mr. Steve Rattner. His appointment was snuck past Congress. He was the 'Car Czar' but didn't even report to the Auto Recovery Czar, who you'll read about soon. Instead, he reports directly to Timothy Geithner, aka Tax Evader.

  Mr. Rattner came to this position with a background in investments. It seems he had a past and was soon under investigation for his handling of the New York State Common Retirement Fund.

It seems some of those under his control made payments to New York State Comptroller Alan Hevesi's political consultant, Hank Morris, as a 'placement agent'. Both Morris and Hevesi were sentenced to prison in 2011.

On April 15, 2010, Quadrangle, Rattner's Corporation, agreed to pay $7 million and cooperate with the Rattner investigation. Rattner agreed to pay $6.2 million and accept a two-year ban from associating with broker-dealers or investment advisers to resolve an SEC probe of kickbacks without admitting or denying any wrongdoing.

There were more suits, one by New York Attorney General Andrew M. Cuomo. In this suit it was alleged Rattner paid undisclosed kickbacks in order to obtain $150 million in investments in Quadrangle from the New York State Common Retirement Fund. In late 2010 Rattner agreed to pay $10 million to settle with the New York Attorney General and will be barred from appearing in any capacity before a public pension fund within the state for five years.

Rattner resigned his position as a Czar. Yet he remains a member of the Council on Foreign Relations, which seems odd since he has only a finance background? His wife Maureen White serves the President as the Senior Advisor on Humanitarian Issues to the Special Representative-Afghanistan and Pakistan for the US State Department. Now that's a mouthful.

There a few things disturbing about this appointment. First the man had no auto experience. Second, the President appoints an Auto Recovery Czar and the Car Czar doesn't report to him or vice versa. Third, the guy is a crook and he gets a top appointment. Why would the President do that?

- Does that bother you?

We now have a Treasury Secretary who doesn't pay taxes and a Car Czar reporting to him who pays settlements to stay out of jail like his coworkers. But it only gets better.

- **Green Jobs Czar:**

  Van Jones was his man in charge of creating 'green jobs'. Of course let's not forget that Mr. Jones has never held a position where he has created even one job let alone enough to justify his salary.

  When Mr. Jones graduated from law school at Yale, he moved to San Francisco. He immediately got involved with an organization known as Standing Together to Organize a Revolutionary Movement, or STORM. STORM was a socialist group whose official Points of Unity upheld revolutionary democracy, revolutionary feminism, and revolutionary internationalism, the central role of the working class, urban Marxism, and Third World Communism. They built connections with other organizations to organize protests, especially against wars and police violence.

Of course, a small aside is that he is a fellow Community Organizer. But isn't he an interesting choice to lead a jobs effort? He resigned amidst scandal.

- Does that bother you?

When you think of Van Jones, think of what you read previously about the history of communism and their goals. Here is a quote from Mr. Jones.

"Right after Rosa Parks refused to give up her seat if the civil rights leaders had jumped out and said, 'OK now we want reparations for slavery, we want redistribution of all the wealth, and we want to legalize mixed marriages.' If we'd come out with a maximum program the very next day, they'd been laughed at. Instead they came out with a very minimum. 'We just want to integrate these buses.'

But, inside that minimum demand was a very radical kernel that eventually meant that from 1964 to 1968 complete revolution was on the table for this country. And, I think that this green movement has to pursue those same steps and stages. Right now we say we want to move from suicidal gray capitalism to something eco-capitalism where at least we're not fast-tracking the destruction of the whole planet. Will that be enough? No, it won't be enough. We want to go beyond the systems of exploitation and oppression altogether. But, that's a process and I think that's what's great about the movement that is beginning to emerge is that the crisis is so severe in terms of joblessness, violence and now ecological threats that people are willing to be both pragmatic and visionary. So the green economy will start off as a small subset and we are going to push it and push it and push it until it becomes the engine for transforming the whole society."

Van Jones
The President's selection as Green Jobs Czar

- **Federal Chief Information Officer of the White House or Info-Tech/Information Czar:**

He selected Mr. Vivek Kundra to oversee all federal technology spending and policy. Mr. Kundra was formerly the Chief Technology Officer for the District of Columbia. We all know what powerhouse technology exists in our Nation's capital city. Can the qualifications get any better? Mr. Kundra was not approved by Congress and his salary not released.

Worth mentioning is that within days of Kundra's appointment to this new Czarist position, as the first Chief Information Officer of the United States, the FBI raided his former employer. Kundra held the position of Chief Technology Officer prior to the FBI raid. They arrested Kundra's former Chief Security Officer and another former employee, for massive fraud and bribes.

The FBI arrested Yusuf Acar, who currently is the District of Columbia's acting chief security officer; police said they found $70,000 in cash in his Washington home. Acar's annual salary is $127,468, according to court documents.

The second suspect arraigned on bribery charges was Sushil Bansal, CEO and founder of Advanced Integrated Technologies Corporation. AITC is a Washington-based outsourcing vendor that has won a number of contracts from the Washington DC's IT department.

AITC is where Vivek Kundra was CEO just a week before his appointment as the Presidents key man for technology for the United States.

Sushil Bansal is on an H-1B guest worker Visa from his native Turkey. He previously worked for DC city government. With an H-1B Visa he is only permitted to work for the employer who sponsored him into the states. Somehow, as an H-1B guest worker Sushil Bansal magically started his own company for which he is now indicted for fraud and bribery by the FBI. He also should be removed from the country for violating his Visa requirement. Perhaps we could find American entrepreneurs to fill these voids in government?

Our new Technology Czar, the very first Chief Information Officer of the United States should have some explaining to do. He was the head of the company. All this was going on and he didn't know? Sound familiar? The President appoints, without Congress, a man with serious questions in his background.

Here is a man who will have all of our government information at his disposal and he has co-workers, under his leadership, involved in illegal activities. He is also outsourcing work overseas. Does this make sense? Even more unbelievable is that Mr. Bansal, a convict, is named entrepreneur of the year by the Association of Indian's in America.

- Does this bother you?

It's worth noting that the President also appointed Aneesh Chopra as Chief Technology Officer or Technology Czar. He also appointed John Holdren as Science and Technology Czar. While Mr. Holdren comes with high marks in science it seems he isn't as strong when it comes to obeying our laws.

In recent hearings before Congress regarding Chinese espionage, Mr. Holdren is being accused of giving our secrets to the Chinese government. He set a meeting with the Chinese to discuss NASA cooperating with the Chinese on their space program. He apparently didn't understand that the People's Liberation Army runs China's space program. Let's look at even more strange Czars.

- **Assistant Secretary for International Affairs and Special Rep for Border Affairs or Border Czar:**

  Alan Bersin is responsible for border security, commerce and trade. He comes highly qualified for such a role, as all of Obama's appointees, since he was formerly on the San Diego County Regional Airport Authority. He once coordinated law enforcement efforts on the border, so I guess he at least knows where it is. Mr. Bersin, unqualified as he is, was not confirmed by Congress and his salary wasn't immediately available.

  What's confusing about this appointment is that we already have a head of US Immigration and Customs Enforcement, John Morton. We also have a head of the US Border Patrol, although I am unable to find the name of the head of that agency. So what is up with this new Czar who reports to Homeland Security Head, Janet Napolitano?

  One of the few things we do know about Mr. Bersin is that he is accused of enforcing a redacting policy on some technology imports that allow fake parts to enter the United States. Bersin is one strange appointment.

- Does this bother you?

It should.

Just ask yourself if his appointment is making a difference on our southern border?

- **Director of Recovery for Auto Communities and Workers or Auto Recovery Czar:**

And that brings us to Ed Montgomery, another appointment with no Congressional Approval and no salary released. While he is the so called 'Auto Recovery Czar' his mandate from Mr. Obama is to cut through the red tape to bring Federal Resources to bear in helping workers and communities impacted by the auto industry's troubles.

Seems like more of a Community Czar to me, but then what do I know. It's clear that he is eminently qualified since he is a former Dean at the University of Maryland. He'd know a lot about government and communities in that job. He also served in the Labor Department under President Clinton.

The bigger question is what responsibility is it of the Fed's to insert their presence in what is a State and Local Government issue? Since when is helping people laid off from work a National issue?

It all seems very community oriented to me. After all, our Presidents background is at the community level. If the only tool you have is a hammer, every problem is a nail. Or perhaps it's just part of Obama's overall plan?

- Does this bother you?

- **Special Assistant to the President and Executive Director of the White House Office of Faith-Based Neighborhood Partnerships or Faith-Based Czar:**

Here's yet another community initiative. That is code for 'vote getter'. You gotta' love this one! Joshua DuBois is the man. I want the job of White House business card title writer. This guy's business card must be the size of a placemat at Denny's if he has his official title on it.

Joshua of course comes from Princeton. He is young and a little light on experience. He is noted as an 'activist', a common trait among most Obama appointees. Think back to what you've learned about the mole that runs from Marxism to Communism to today. That mole is starting to smell.

What exactly Joshua will do for his $98,000 a year salary is unclear? He leads a council of 25 unnamed, 'influential' leaders to help establish and nurture programs at the community level. Once again I ask, "Since when is the 'doing' of community work a federal government responsibility? The answer is since Obama took over.

Back in the fifties and early sixties when I went to school I was taught my United States of America was a group of federalist states. The federal government intervened only when the issues were for the greater good, interstate commerce or national defense.

Now we have a guy who breezes into office, appointing countless people to totally new positions; circumventing Congress every time he can. And many Americans think it's all good? It's not!

The appointment of a Faith Based Czar seems to conflict with a President who cancelled the National Day of Prayer? How can we not have prayer in public schools but the new kid in town appoints 'faith-based' Czar to work at the local level. It all smells a little like an ACORN to me.

- Does this bother you?

You keep thinking back to those communist goals we discussed and you'll see the bridge the communists are building getting stronger and stronger.

- **Deputy Assistant to the President and Director of the Office of Urban Affairs or Urban Czar:**

"Could we have another Denny's placemat please"? What a title for Adolfo Carrion Jr. He was not confirmed by Congress but he does make the tidy sum of $158,500 a year. His role is to guide Federal investment in US cities. He is to focus on job creation, housing and efficient spending. One more 'vote getter' for the President.

Mr. Carrion Jr. comes to us with the usual political and community background. Absent are any real jobs or experience that would denote an ability to deliver on the requirements of this job.

The group Citizens for Responsibility and Ethics sent a letter asking for Attorney General Eric Holder to request a Department of Justice investigation in to New York Daily News reports on Mr. Carrion Jr. They allege a pay-to-play scheme in his background. Apparently nothing ever happened with the Department of Justice request. It would also seem nothing is happening with the Urban Czar's jobs and housing responsibility.

- Does this bother you?

Does any of this make you wonder who was performing these duties prior to these new appointments? You should think about that and why so many of these new jobs are focused at the community level. What did Saul Alinsky teach about that? Why is the federal government suddenly so minutely involved in local communities?

- **Associate General Counsel and Chief Diversity Officer or Federal Communication Commission Diversity Czar:**

Mark Lloyd is tasked with, well, we're not sure. There is currently a head of the FCC so it seems odd that both he and Mr. Lloyd hold similar positions reporting to the same guy? But while Mr. Lloyd is a former broadcaster and communications attorney, he is well, just a wee bit controversial at times. As with Van Jones, he's a real peach of an American patriot. Mr. Lloyd is so left leaning he makes Harry Reid look like a diehard conservative.

While his background would fit a normal size business card, his views on democracy certainly won't. One of his many beliefs led him to propose fees on privately held radio stations to provide funding for publicly held radio competitors, ala PBS. Mr. Lloyd, in his 2006 book, called Thomas Jefferson's quote, "That government is best which governs least", outdated.

But the one you gotta' love is his comments regarding Hugo Chavez, the current Dictator and Thug from Venezuela, our newest terrorist state to the south.

Mr. Lloyd praised President Chavez for his 'incredible' attainment of a democratic revolution. Keep in mind that the revolution he is praising closed over 200 Venezuelan radio stations and the guy praising him is atop our own Federal Communications Commission.

- Does this bother you?

A long time ago, back in 1965, as a young Marine, I was wounded fighting in Santo Domingo, Dominican Republic. I was wounded fighting to take back the radio station from the revolutionaries.

That is an important goal of revolutionaries. They first want to control communications to the people. I hope we can take our radio stations back before this guy gets control. I hope there is no bloodshed like we experienced in the Dominican Republic. But that is no longer guaranteed.

You cannot sit out this election. Our very freedom depends on it. Think back to the communist goals. Open your eyes to what is happening in America. It is that important!

- **Special Envoy for Eurasian Energy or Eurasian Energy Czar:**

Richard Morningstar is this dude's name, and he is to provide advice to the Secretary of State on strategic and energy relations in Europe. Which for Mr. Morningstar means Russia and Central Asia? Countries like Uzbekistan, Kazakhstan, Turkmenistan and Mongolia.

We have a massive energy department to handle energy but Obama needs this guy? The US Department of Energy was established in 1977 by then President Jimmy Carter. Oil prices have continued to increase and our dependence on foreign oil is worse than ever. The DOE today has over 16,000 employees and over 93,000 contract workers. Their annual budget is over $27 billion a year. Why on earth do we need Mr. Morningstar and his $420,750 annual salary?

I know none of us have seen a drop in the price at the pump. We haven't seen our dependence on foreign oil drop. What we have seen is our President commit $3 billion to Brazil for off shore drilling that he doesn't allow in the United States. Makes you wonder since the oil coming offshore in Brazil will be heading to China? As you struggle to buy groceries this week and fill up the family's eight year old car, how are you feeling about this guy on our payroll making nearly half a million dollars? I'm upset and hope you are too.

- Does this bother you?

- **Czars, Czars and More Czars:**

There is a common thread that runs through these appointments. First, most have no real working experience. They are academics, activists, community organizers or politicians leaning to the Left. Secondly, a careful peak under the covers shows they are socialists.

As I go down a list of other Czars appointed by Obama, be sure to ask yourself, why? President Obama has appointed 33 Czars, more than any other President before him. Here we go:

- Coordinator for Arms Control and Nonproliferation or Nonproliferation Weapons of Mass Destruction Czar.

- Director of White House Office of Energy and Climate Change Policy or Global- Warming Czar.

- Intellectual Property Enforcement Coordinator or Copyright Czar.

- Assistant to the President for Homeland Security and Counterterrorism or Counterterrorism Czar.

- Deputy Secretary of the Department of the Interior or California Water Czar.

- Director of Office of National AIDS Policy or AIDS Czar.

- Cyber Security Czar.

- Safe-Schools Czar.

- Great Lakes Czar.

- Economic Recovery Czar.

- Guantanamo Closure Czar.

- Salary/Pay Compensation Czar.

- International Climate Czar.

- Global Warming Czar.

- Afghanistan and Pakistan Czar.

- Sudan Czar.

- Mideast Peace Czar.

Can you imagine our country is going down the tubes financially while our President adds all these people to 'new' jobs in his administration? It's hard to comprehend. Look at this list and think, really think. Think back to the communist goals of the late 60's and Saul Alinsky's teachings and connect the dots. They connect very easily.

There are other Czars under consideration believe it or not. Check these out:

- Health Choices Czar.

- Special Advisor to the Secretary of State on Biofuels.

Can you imagine a staff meeting with Obama and his Czars? It must be like the Annual Convention of Monkeys with Guns. He must go to bed at night laughing his ass off with the First Lady, in disbelief that he's getting away with this scam and it's so easy.

- Does any of this bother you?

There is one reason you put this many people on the payroll over and above your normal chain of command. You don't trust the department leaders and you want the inside scoop as to what is going on in your administration. If he were a leader, that wouldn't be a problem.

If all those Czars weren't enough, we've saved the very best for last.

- **The Greatest Czar of All is not a Czar at All:**

In fairness, His Highness, Mr. Obama doesn't call her a Czar. I am. And more interestingly, most of his staff, including his Czars, doesn't like the lady the President calls, "His closest friend".

Her name is Valerie Jarrett. Of course she hails from Chicago, home of some of the Nation's most notorious political shenanigans, Saul Alinsky and headquarters to the Communist Party USA.

Admittedly, every President has close confidants and advisors. That's nothing new. President Obama has Valerie, a former Chicago real estate executive, as his closest sidekick. He says he runs 'every' decision by her. Her official title needs a jumbo Denny's placemat. It reads, 'Senior Advisor and Special Assistant to the President for Intergovernmental Affairs and Public Engagement'. Tell me how you manage someone with that job description?

Ms. Jarrett was responsible for championing Green-Jobs Czar Van Jones, to the White House. That worked out real well, eh? And she championed the position and the person of FCC Diversity Czar, Mark Lloyd. He is a tragedy waiting to happen. She was also behind the President's disastrous visit to Copenhagen to pitch Chicago before the International Olympic Committee. And I thought it was three strikes and you're out?

There's also an unnamed report that put her in the middle of the decision to take out Osama. Guess what?

The unconfirmed report says she was against taking him out? If that's true, it's just a bit scary to me and should be to you that literally an old friend is in the middle of national security issues. The New York Times reported one political operative as saying, "there are only two people in this world the President will never say no to. One of them is named Michelle".

- Does this bother you?

So there you have it, the New Sheriff in Town and part of his New, Approved and Unapproved Posse'. So what do you think? What do his selections say about him? I taught my kids that they will become like those they run around with. Who is our President running around with? You decide. To me it looks like a group of socialist carrying out a long range plan.

What these choices mean is that Obama is part of the one-world-government crowd. He uses community organizers to drive his change in America. His change is to move America to socialism. He has strategically placed people in positions to drive services into areas where more Americans will be dependent on the government.

Unfortunately, we could go on forever with our Presidents new Posse' but we'll transition to more signs of the mole deep inside our society.

There are three important points on his choices for Cabinet and personal assistants or Czars:

1. Obama's choice of people reveals a great deal about his character. He is loyal to the change he set out to bring and the people he needs to make it happen. Those people range from sixties radicals to the one-world-government crowd.

He is not loyal to the US Constitution that he swore to uphold. He is loyal to what he and his cronies think we need. And that is a one-world government, under socialism at best and communism at worst.

2. While America is being destroyed, our news media cheers and supports the man they made. Mr. Hardball, Chris Matthews, was on his knees rolling questions to him on the ground, not playing hardball at all.

   The old media, NBC, CBS and ABC, are a non-factor today because their bias in unquestionable. The media is a huge part of the problem. Even *60 Minutes* is a set up. They treat him like the greatest 4th greatest President we've ever seen. His words not mine.

2. If you step back and look at what is really going on in this country under this President, you will see the enemy is now within. The enemy wants us bound by the United Nations. The enemy is this administration. Obama is not responsible for getting us here, but he is responsible to move the socialist plan forward as fast as he possible can.

3. He is the finisher, coming in the ninth inning to win the game. The time has come to think seriously about the country and lifestyle we are leaving our children and grandchildren. It isn't the smog from cars, global warming or the amount of waste we generate that is going to get us. It is the enemy within.

4. It's not oil sands, gay rights or the fat at McDonalds, as Al Gore and Michael Moore contend, that is going to get us.

Those things are luxuries we in the civilized world can choose to make into causes and march in the street over but they aren't the real issues we face.

In Somalia, or Afghanistan or any of the 'stans for that matter, they would laugh at us for being concerned about global warming, while they're starving. Those things are all distractions that force us to take our eye off the ball. The ball is the American dream, and it is being stolen by our enemy within. We know it has happened before in our history, and it is happening right now.

Barrack Hussein Obama is the finisher in the game where the American Dream is being destroyed. He has a lot of help. One of the biggest drivers in our move to socialism and a one world government is George Soros. We talked about him earlier.

Think Obama isn't a socialist? In a speech delivered at Osawatomie High School in Osawatomie, Kansas, on Tuesday, December 6, 2011 the President argued that while a limited government that preserves free markets "speaks to our rugged individualism" as Americans, such a system "doesn't work" and "has never worked" and that Americans must look to a more activist government that taxes more, spends more and regulates more if they want to preserve the middle class.

Obama said, "Now, it's a simple theory. And we have to admit, it's one that speaks to our rugged individualism and our healthy skepticism of too much government. That's in America's DNA. And that theory fits well on a bumper sticker. But here's the problem: It doesn't work.

It has never worked." So you see he doesn't think America ever worked. That's why he is all about change.

He went on to say, "It didn't work when it was tried in the decade before the Great Depression. It's not what led to the incredible postwar booms of the '50s and '60s. And it didn't work when we tried it during the last decade. I mean, understand, it's not as if we haven't tried this theory".

Obama is taking us down. He doesn't even hide it anymore. It is up to you and me to stop that from happening. We must act now. We must convince others to act now. The first step to stopping this travesty is to remove our current President from office in 2012.

Read on as we take a look at the President's very first initiative ... Healthcare.

"That government is best which governs the least, because its people discipline themselves."

Thomas Jefferson

"Human dignity is bound up with taking responsibility for conducting one's own affairs."

Paul Rahe

"Let us with caution indulge the supposition that morality can be maintained without religion. Reason and experience both forbid us to expect that national morality can prevail in exclusion of religious principle".

George Washington

Healthcare, Whether You Want it or Not

President Obama had a couple of issues to deal with on healthcare. First were his campaign promises. Second was his need to have more Americans than ever dependent on the government, otherwise known as Socialism. His agenda was at stake.

As we look at Obama's healthcare plan, there are two things to consider. First, the healthcare plan itself. That is, if we can figure out exactly what is in the new healthcare reform bill? Our Congressmen don't know. Our Senators don't know. We know Mr. President didn't read it. They all said it was 'too big' to read. Imagine that?

The second item for discussion is exactly why push it through, since the bill didn't solve a single healthcare problem in America. It created more problems than it solved, it didn't give us 'national' health care and it will break the bank. So why did our President cram it down our throats? We'll discuss them in order.

Let's look at the bill. When we began this charade, there were the likes of Michael Moore, Al Gore, Nancy Pelosi, Harry Reid and the President himself touted the advantages of what they then called national healthcare. There was even mention of England and Canada as examples that it could be done.

I happen to have a few friends in England, so I checked on how they liked it. The result was somewhat mixed, but I'd say overall they were happy with what they had. The one fellow's wife was a Pharmacist who worked in the States for a few years. I actually met them in Fort Benning, Georgia. He emailed me and said, "My wife said not to worry, the drug lobby in the US will never let what we have in England into America." And she was right on that count.

My second look into national healthcare came from my personal experiences in Canada. In my 40 plus years traveling there, I've had occasion to use the services of the Sudbury Regional Medical Center, a mere 80-mile drive from our former cottage.

Let me share a few experiences I've had with national healthcare:

- My first experience dates back to the mid-eighties when a Marine veteran, who served with me in Nam, was visiting from Long Island with his family.

  One of his boys fell and broke his arm. He speeds to Sudbury at around 80 or 85 miles per hour and is stopped by an OPP Officer, that's Ontario Provincial Police. He explains what is happening and the Officer says, "Follow me!" and races him to the hospital.

  He was immediately treated and released. Although he was an American, there was no charge. That was impressive.

- A couple years later, now in the late 80's I had a similar experience. I broke my hand and was treated and released with no charge.

- Now, let's fast forward to around 2005, fifteen years since my last visit. I'm a guy with kidney stone problems and had an attack at the cottage. My wife and I took off, but the pain was overwhelming. My wife called On-Star. They talked an ambulance to us as we drove. We met and transferred, and they took me to the hospital.

I received no treatment or medication in the ambulance! My pain was a 10 but they said they weren't paid to give me medication. For their services, I received a $400 invoice. It would have been cheaper to stay in my Suburban.

My wife and I sat in a little emergency room by ourselves for 4 hours. My wife finally tracked down a nurse. She asked her for a Doctor. She replied, "Ma'am there are no Doctors here tonight. They all moved to the States, there's no money up here." We gave up and left. We received a bill for $630.00.

- In 2009 we raced to Sudbury Regional one more time. I choked with what turned out to be an esophageal blockage. It was awful. The EMT's were called once again and delivered me to the hospital amidst constant choking.

The ambulance ride was now $550.00 and they did not administer to me at all. This time they said they'd take me to someone who made a lot more money than they did.

To make a long and painful story short, we sat in that little room again in emergency for 9 hours. Yes, I said 9 hours. It was 9 hours of retching without treatment. At 4 AM, a Doctor came in to get me for the operation. He apologized and said, "All the Doctors moved to the States with you guys." He did operate, and I was back at the cottage by 7 AM the next day. All I was told, "You had an esophageal blockage." I left there $3,600.00 poorer.

- On the way home from Canada I choked again while eating lunch in Decatur, Illinois. Armed with my recent memories of esophageal blockages we headed for the nearest emergency room. It was the Decatur Memorial Hospital. It was in fact the exact same problem.

  I walked in the ER hacking like a coal miner with black lung disease and looking pretty bad as well. A Doctor immediately gave me a shot to stop my coughing, and an hour later they operated. While doing so they expanded my throat to prevent the problem happening again. It was simple.

I'm using Canada as an example because I happen to have experience there. From the time I first experienced national healthcare in Canada until 2009, the care had deteriorated dramatically while the costs went up.

Under government healthcare, these are the things we'll be looking forward to. I learned that Doctors in Canada are paid on a per patient basis, once a year. The Doctors keep records and send them to the Province annually. They're paid based on individuals, not visits. So if you see Mrs. Smith 42 times this year it counts as one. Sure makes me want to spend 10 to 12 years in medical school to become a Doctor.

National healthcare does not work the way our healthcare does today. Our government has destroyed Social Security, Fannie Mae and Freddie Mac and we want to give our healthcare to them? Our crisis in America is not health services, it is cost. The cost of healthcare in America is driven by the drug companies, the lawyers and insurance companies. After studying all that, I realized the behemoth of a bill they produced for our healthcare wasn't national healthcare at all.

We want to turn over control of all health care to a government that handed out over $98 billion in improper Medicare payments in 2009. Enron executives went to jail for defrauding investors of less than a half of one percent of that total.

What Obama came up with was a program that forced all Americans to buy insurance. We have the right to 'buy' insurance now. We can't afford it. How is that national healthcare? It will put Doctors on a limited income and make patient beds scarce. His massive redo of healthcare, if implemented, will serve to further degrade the state of our Nation's finances, as well as its healthcare.

It will further feed the likes of golden boy, sleazy John Edwards. Edwards made his fame and fortune fleecing others in personal injury and medical malpractice lawsuits. He won millions of dollars in the name of poor people everywhere. I'll bet you less than 50 cents on the dollar of those settlements went to the people John Edwards and his kind represent.

The nation has a problem with healthcare. The problem needs to be addressed in Congress. Congress is filled with lawyers and lobbyist. Therefore it is never going to be addressed until we throw most of the bums out.

That leads me to my second point in this chapter. Why, since the bill didn't solve a single problem in healthcare, would our President jam it down our collective throats? Remember, he, Reid and Pelosi shut the doors and wrote the legislation all alone. Our President, Mr. Togetherness during his campaign, showed his true colors as a 'divider'.

Virginia Attorney General Ken Cuccinelli is challenging the federal government on the healthcare bill. He has challenged the President before.

The Attorney General said, "Attorneys General are the last line of defense, when there are no principle protectors of the Constitution in Washington. We've been called on from a federalist posture ... to step up on behalf of our states, to restrain the federal government and keep it within its enumerated powers. And we've been doing that."

We need to consider the possibility that the President is testing the waters of just how far he could go in usurping the states' authority. The healthcare reform bill is just a means to an end. Not a very good end for Americans. The final stanza of this song will be written, I believe to his surprise, by the United States Supreme Court. Is the healthcare bill constitutional? We'll find out before the election.

We cannot take this lightly. Why is this important to every American? Consider the following points:

- If the President can set a precedent for requiring Americans to purchase one thing, like health insurance; he can do it for anything.

- If he gets more people dependent on the Federal government, more people are apt to keep him and those like him in office because they depend on the government.

- The bigger government gets, the less freedom its citizens retain.

- All of the 3 points above dovetail into communist goals set around 1960.

- The Presidents tactics and actions match those of his mentor, Saul Alinsky.

We must not just listen to his words. We must watch his actions and compare. Remember, Candidate Obama was all about transparency and being the leader who brings people together, not a divider who pulls them apart. Remember that? He made a big deal about Bush the Younger's polarizing impact on American politics.

Yet, as we previously mentioned, during the Healthcare run up and the drafting of the bill, the Democratic leadership, under the direction of our President, completely shut the Republicans out of the process. Because of our President, they had no say in the drafting of the healthcare legislation. It was old fashioned Chicago style politics at its best, with a little Marxism thrown in.

- Does that bother you?

To top all of that are the paybacks and exemptions from participating that already issued. The first payback was given to Nebraska. It's referred to as the Cornhusker Kickback and came as a result of Nebraska Senator's helping with the passage of the bill. For their votes Harry Reid insured a stipulation in the bill that Nebraska's Medicaid funding would be covered 100% by the federal government.

What about exemptions from participating in the health care bill? It started with McDonalds, then came the United Federation of Teachers and now several states are getting an exemption. I might add several Republican Governors have been turned down for exemptions. Now that's a great healthcare plan.

You must not sit out the 2012 elections. We cannot re-elect President Barack Hussein Obama. Study his actions not his words. Study the changes he is making. Look at what we learned from healthcare, you cannot challenge the new President. He is the Emperor and expects his word to not ever be challenged.

"Associate with men of good quality if you esteem your own reputation; for it is better to be alone than in bad company."

George Washington

*"When there is a bill that ends up on my desk
as the president, you the public will have five minutes
to look online and find out what's in it before I sign it."*

President Barack Hussein Obama

*"Arbitrary power is most easily established
on the ruins of liberty abused to licentiousness."*

George Washington

Dissent Not Welcome Here

In a Houston Chronicle article on June 2, 2011, Bill Hammond writes, "There are enough examples of the Obama Administration tearing down Texas to make the David Letterman Top Ten List." That wouldn't be too hard for Letterman, who slobbers all over the President like he's in love. Hammond goes on to say, "But, there's really nothing funny about the full frontal assault that's come out of Washington against our state in recent months."

I mentioned his arrogance on the issue of immigration in a previous chapter. Announcing our borders are safer than ever, while Governor Perry and Greta Van Susterin are reporting live on TV from family farms overrun by drug smuggling illegals. Just as in the case of Arizona, where he and his Mexican cohort, Calderon, sue the state, he is trying to tear Texas down too. Why would he do that?

In his article, Mr. Harmon reports, "The moves against Texas are well documented, some are more brazen than others, and they amount to a war by regulation and executive orders aimed at knocking Texas off its leadership position."

If you want to know all you have to do is watch the news as it pertains to Texas and the White House. We know he and his administration don't like Bush the Younger, or the Older for that matter. But singling out the leading business state for the seventh year in a row, as named by Chief Executives magazine, is a bit much. The way things are going for the President and his economic recovery, you'd think he'd want to learn from the best, the creator of jobs and a strong economy, Texas.

My family and I weren't born in Texas but we did live there twice, in Houston and Dallas. We feel like the bumper sticker we saw one day after moving to Dallas that said, 'I wasn't born a Texan but I got here as fast as I could'.

We enjoyed living there, heat and all. Their housing is priced fair, there's no state income tax and the business atmosphere is outstanding. We were proud to send our kids to school and have them sing the Eyes of Texas right before the Pledge of Allegiance each morning.

I've heard it said there are two ways to have the tallest building in town. One was is to build it, the way Texas has done. The other way is to go around and knock everyone else's building down, that is the Obama Way, its Bush's fault.

If you look at the ratings by the CEO's Mr. Obama's home state of Illinois is ranked 48th, while his other partner in crime New York is ranked 49th. The state in the most trouble, the one where Obama appointed a Federal Water Czar to help, California, is ranked 50th. Apparently for California, water wasn't the problem!

So Mr. Obama has proven he is a great 'knocker down' of opponent's buildings. As well as states and people who oppose him. Let's look at a couple of Scuds lobbed Texas way since Barry took the helm:

1. The controversial move to pass over Mission Control and the Johnson Space Center for the home of the retired space shuttle. Shucks they didn't do anything but run the program there from its inception.

2. Then a very controversial decision to suddenly switch production of military tactical vehicles after 17 years from Sealy, Texas BAE plant to where, union heavy Wisconsin. That certainly couldn't have anything to do with those unions now would it? Ask South Carolina, another right-to-work state, where the President is after Boeing, trying to force them not put their plant in a right-to-work state.

3. The best one may be the US Fish and Wildlife Service which is acting to protect the 3-inch Dunes Sagebrush Lizard by putting it on the endangered species list. If they do, it will shut down oil and gas production in the affected West Texas counties surrounding Midland and Odessa.

   If you know anything about Texas, while having outstanding high school football, Midland and Odessa are like the Middle East of American oil.
   The really interesting thing about this is that next door in New Mexico, the same administration, wanting to shut down oil production in Texas, made agreements with companies and landlords to work together to preserve the lizards habitat while work went on.

4. Add these key items to the immigration issue and it makes you wonder once again, just what America Mr. Obama is President of?

He's sure not Presidential if you tick him off or disagree with him. He is on a mission, and not the kind of mission America usually charges off on. The fact he is called the 'Messiah' by the American press is fitting. He has shown time and again that one of his character flaws is his blame game. He blamed George the Younger for torturing prisoners, which they did on a limited basis. Voila'! When they knocked off Osama he had to admit that it was the result of intelligence received as part of a water boarding interrogation.
He blames George the Younger for the economy and certainly some of it is. How about the fact a democratically controlled Congress blocked Bush's attempt to bring Fannie Mae under control. Did I hear the names of Barney Frank and Chris Dodd? There are two stalwart leaders of the Democratic Party for you.

Believe me; I don't like either party today. I think we need a third party alternative and then clean out both the House and Senate. But we must understand that Obama will blame anyone but himself. He's like a little kid who can never be wrong.

I get my news from Jon Stewart on the Daily Show, but Fox is a legitimate network. They recently refused ad's that were negative of Obama. Yes they're on the right, CNN and MSNBC are on the left and the Big Three are out to lunch. None of that justifies a President to boycott one network, Fox.

Does anything give a President, the right to block access to a network because he thinks they're off base? My goodness, George the Younger wouldn't have been able to have a news conference if that were the case. Everyone attacked him. So what is it with the Presidents thin skin?

In October, 2009, the Administration denied they were trying to cut Fox News from an interview with Treasury official, Kenneth Feinberg. A Treasury spokesman denied the charge and alleged they had the same opportunity as the other networks. Then, at the very last minute they were included.

The organization Judicial Watch, doing their job, obtained administration emails on the subject of Fox through a public records request. What they found is disturbing. Deputy Communications Director Jennifer Psaki called Fox News Anchor Bret Baier, a 'lunatic'. Then she went on to say, "I am putting some dead fish in his cubby, just cause!" That was right adult of Ms. Psaki.

They also found a White House Press Officer wrote that we, "Demonstrated our willingness and ability to exclude Fox News from significant interference." So that's free speech in our new President's White House. Remember, 'take the radio station first'.

Here is a Harvard Law grad, a former organizer on the streets of Chicago, a former State and US Senator and now President of the United States, why would he be scared of Fox News? Because it is the only network he doesn't have in his back pocket. Obama has an anti-Fox crusade whether he admits it or not.

Obama mouthpiece David Axelrod charged that Fox is 'not a real news network'. White House Communications Director Anita Dunn attacked Fox News for being a wing of the Republican Party. Former Fox host Glenn Beck, released a video of Dunn singing praises for Chinese Dictator and record setting murderer, Mao Tse tung. She called Mao one of her 'favorite political philosophers'. Just makes your knees want to buckle. Remember, you become like those around you ... and he chose each of them.

There was an attempt at reconciliation between Roger Ailes, President of Fox News and the President. The Washington Post reported that in one heated exchange Roger Ailes told the President, " If you're asking me if we're going to be 'in the tank' for you, like MSNBC and CNN, the answer is no!"

Obama was upset with Hannity's report on Bill Ayers the terrorist, who Obama claimed to barely know. Hannity's report showed the clear connections between the two, and the President took exception. During the campaign Obama denied ever having a kick off fund raising meeting at Ayers house when he first ran for Illinois Senate. Ayer was captured on tape in late 2011 speaking to a crowd and joking about having Obama's Illinois Senate kickoff at his home.

As the Fox war heated up, Al Hunt from Bloomsburg TV, asked Anita Dunn, the Mao lover, pointedly about where all this was coming from. She replied, "I am not one who is known for going rogue". That is PC Speak for 'I've been directed to do this Fox assassination'.

Next was the campaign to 'encourage' subject matter experts from appearing on Fox News. MoveOn.org, that wonderfully democratic George Soros organization, circulated petitions to Democratic members of Congress to 'not appear on Fox News'.

New York Daily News Bureau Chief Thomas DeFrank said, "I can never remember a White House urging a news organization to boycott other news organizations. That strikes me as unprecedented". Yet, we haven't heard much on this from Katie Couric or Brian Williams. They don't even pick up on big Fox News stories until they're mainstream news. Why is that do you suppose?

The Los Angeles Times reported that an unidentified Democratic strategist appeared on Fox News; soon after he received a call from a White House official telling him, "We better not see you on Fox again". Respected journalist Charles Krauthammer wrote, "The current White House wants to delegitimize any significant dissent." I bet that's in some of those Karl Marx and Saul Alinsky writings?

The war between Obama and Fox started from the sparks set off by Fox exposing the ACORN scandal. We've all heard enough of those particulars, ACORN helping people with prostitution, avoiding the IRS and a few other illegal acts. Who is ACORN? It's an organization President Barack once represented as a lawyer. It is an organization he partnered with for Project Vote where he registered 150,000 new voters. And I'll bet all of those voters were legal--you can't see me winking but I am.

The issue of ACORN is again an issue of credibility and character. The Washington Times reported that Obama conducted leadership training sessions for ACORN. Candidate Obama's Campaign paid an outfit known as Citizens Consulting Inc. $832,000 for get-out-to-vote initiatives.

It's worth noting that Citizens Consulting Inc. is the umbrella organization that directs most of ACORN funding. It may just be me, but don't you think the evidence would seem to indicate the Barackmeister knew something about ACORN?

His remarks speak to his character first hand. While talking with George Stephanopoulos, the President went back to one of his most popular tactics of being above it all. When asked by Stephanopoulos about the matter the President replied, "You know. Frankly, it's not really something I've followed closely. I didn't even know ACORN got Federal funding." Do you really believe that he knew nothing after hearing his background with the organization listed above?

When he made the above statement, only Fox tried to follow up. That statement ranks up there with some of our most notorious Presidents. Take President Richard Nixon denying Watergate. Bill Clinton gave us, "I did not have sex with that woman" and "I did not inhale. Now Barack says, "You know, frankly, it's not really something I've followed closely. I didn't even know ACORN got Federal funding." He is a living, breathing travesty.

If that isn't bad enough, President Obama's own stimulus package, Section 261, provides $15 billion in taxpayer funding to organizations just like ACORN. The Department of Housing and Urban Development awarded $79,819 to the Miami Branch of ACORN Housing Group. That is the new name of ACORN since their troubles with Fox News began.

When the US Chamber of Commerce came out against Obama's plan for creating a financial protection agency for investors, they soon found themselves at the receiving end of Obama's whip. He came out and called their ads 'completely false' and questioned whether they were still representing American businesses.

Those are the comments of our President when it came to The US Chamber of Commerce? Why attack them? He does it simply because they challenged him.

There is a very common thread in Obama's behavior. He sat for 20 years in the Reverend Wright's church listening to anti-American screaming but claims he didn't hear a thing. When controversy erupted, he dropped the Right Reverend faster than followers of Jim and Tammy Faye dropped them. He conveniently doesn't remember anything about ACORN, although he represented them as a lawyer. He served on the Board of the Woods Fund with terrorist Bill Ayers. At that time Ayers held a fundraiser in his house for Obama, but doesn't know Ayers or remember the fundraiser.

Our President is a fake, a very good one, but a fake. He is all for change but not what the change American people signed up for. He becomes frustrated when he doesn't get his way. He's a narcissist and he's dangerous. He must go in 2012.

In June, 2011, Dale McFeathers of Scripps Howard News wrote a short article entitled, "An Entourage Surpassing the Queen's". He is referring to our President's arrival in London for the G-20 Summit. He is the President of our United States and deserves to be protected. It is a tough world out there today. In America we are facing some serious, I mean some serious, economic issues. None of that seems to matter to Mr. Obama.

As reported in Great Britain, Obama arrived with a staff of 500. That included 200 Secret Service agents, a team of 6 Doctors, the White House Chef and kitchen staff and all the President's own food. By golly Mr. Clampett, you are important.

That's not the best part. The Evening Standard reported he came with 35 vehicles, 4 speech writers and 12 Teleprompter's. As Mr. McFeathers said, "For sure, our President is not going to be at a loss for words."

He also brought Marine One, the chopper that ferries him around. That isn't abnormal but it was only a short hop from Stansted Airport to London. I'm surprised he couldn't use the Brit's super duper chopper?

In addition to Marine One, they brought several decoy Marine Ones to insure that no one knew which chopper he was on. Maybe in our world today that's cool? The Brit's were repulsed by his show of extravagance. Are you?

At a time our country is going down the tubes in more ways than one, Mr. President has to travel in style. And not only just to the G-20. Consider the cost to taxpayers when Obama decided to take Michelle on a date to New York City. Just for the evening. Don't you wish you and your wife could do that for a date?

Imagine the inconvenience it is to the community where they dine? Streets are blocked off, the Secret Service is everywhere, traffic is shut down and the airport is cleared out when Air Force One comes and goes. Wouldn't you suppose there's a quaint little place near the White House they could go? Apparently they haven't found one worthy of their honor.

How about all those vacations to Hawaii? We'd all love going out there. When he goes there the hotel suite costs us taxpayers $50,000 a week. I wonder if he and Michelle stayed there when he was a Community Organizer. Or even as a Senator? He didn't write those two best sellers about himself until he was running for the Big House. We now have American Royalty whether we like it or not.

We never hear much about him and the misses returning to the old neighborhood. You know, back in Chicago, in the 'hood, where they got their humble start. He and Michelle never actually lived in those communities they were organizing. Nope.

They lived in beautiful Hyde Park. A community organized by the Rockefeller's back in the day. The Obama's really should share their economic success secrets with the rest of us. It literally could turn the country around if we rocketed to the top like they did. It's just amazing.

He travels often and well, as in super expensive trips, all at a time our country is drowning in debt, most of it to our enemies.

- Does any of this bother you?

Please say yes. Our freedom and country depend on it. We must wake up from our complacency. We must open our eyes, get out of bed and get to work making a difference.

We're now going to delve into the President's policy on immigration, the one where he promotes the illegal immigration of the United States of America. Why would he do that?

*"For all the noise and anger that too often surrounds
the immigration debate, America has nothing to fear
from today's immigrants. They have come here
for the same reason that families have always come
here--for the hope that in America, they could build
a better life for themselves and their families.
Like the waves of immigrants that came before them
and the Hispanic Americans whose families have been
here for generations, the recent arrival of
Latino immigrants will only enrich our country."*

President Barack Hussein Obama

"The right of a nation to kill a tyrant in case of necessity can no more be doubted than to hang a robber, or kill a flea."

John Adams

The President Who Sues His States

President Obama's positions are scary. His stance on illegal immigration is even scarier and is another piece in the puzzle of the new world order. Let's take a closer look at this new piece in Obama's puzzle.

The illegal immigration problem came along before the Obama Administration. The problem reaches back a few presidencies. What makes our new Sheriff a little terrifying is that, once again, he sides with the international community? Who would have ever dreamed a sitting President would side with the President of Mexico in a lawsuit against one of our own states--Arizona? Not me!

But sue Arizona he did. Why? Say what you want, but Governor Jan Brewer of Arizona simply passed state legislation that would allow them to do what the Federal government wouldn't do, enforce current immigration laws. There is great debate over this one and I'm not sure why. Maybe I'm too simple. We have Federal laws that it is illegal to come into this country without proper processing. That is not up for debate and never has been. The US Supreme Court will finally decide who is right.

When I recently traveled to Canada, I needed a Passport. When I recently traveled to the Dominican Republic, I needed my Passport and a Visa from their government. A few hikers from America strayed into Iran, and they spent a couple of years in some very bad jails because they were in the country illegally. Try going into North Korea, Pakistan, India or Russia; no can do. Try going into Mexico illegally, and see what happens. So why would our President stand beside Felipe Calderon, Mexico's President, when it came to Governor Brewer? What does that say about him?

I don't know about you, but that bothers me. I'm not against immigration as long as it is legal. And I know it's a real problem. Think of it this way.

Imagine the United States was your physical home. And let's say, being America, you have a large home, maybe four bedrooms. You and your spouse have only one child. The three of you are living peacefully, getting by in your home called America.

Your life is fine, until one night, someone knocks on your door. A little scared, you go downstairs and check it out. You carefully open the door to find a bedraggled looking man, woman and small child. They could be any nationality, that's not the issue. They are standing at your door and now you have a problem.

The people on your door speak very limited English. They're motioning that they want you to let them in. You try to explain to them that you'll call your local church, the YMCA or the Salvation Army, maybe they can help. They don't understand and insist on coming in.

After a few frustrating minutes they leave, dejected and walk away. The experience left you unnerved. You're scared for your family but feel bad for the people. Back upstairs, you talk it over with your wife and fall asleep feeling guilty. After a sleepless night, you awake to find the three people from the night before sleeping in a shed in your back yard.

You speak with them, but, unable to communicate, you finally call the Police. The Police come and inform you that there is nothing they can do. Their hands are tied. You go to work perplexed at your situation. You return from work, and your new, uninvited guests are still in your shed. Your wife has been feeding them.

You awaken the next morning to find two more immigrants in your backyard. You can't afford to keep them, but you do feel bad. The next morning a few more arrive. But the new faces aren't as friendly as the original folks. The new crew talks and acts tough. You now fear for the safety of your family.

You call the police who inform you that unless they actually commit a crime, their hands are tied by immigration laws. They leave and the toughs inform you they are moving into one of your spare bedrooms, like it or not. Before long they fill all your rooms, your basement, living room, your entire house. Your small child and wife live in fear, and there is nothing you can do about it. You're expected to get them to school just like your child and pay their medical bills just like your family. The government says there is nothing you can do.

That my friends, is America today! You can play this one out yourself. In a few days, you've got a new baby in the house, who is now a US citizen the easy way. Certainly not what our grandfathers had to do for permanence in the United States. But it is happening right now, today.

Before you can say 'Barrack Hussein Obama', today's illegal immigrants are on food stamps, eating better than your family, enjoying free medical and having babies who are immediately United States citizens. If you live in California, their life is even better.

The problem with our imaginary home is that the homeowner will soon run out of money. He may even try and toss the people out of his house. Remember, he can't, because it is against our laws, or so they say. That house is Arizona and Texas and all the other Border States right now. The Federal government will not let them stop anyone from coming into their house, and fights them when they want to kick anyone out.

In real life Obama recently put a hold on 300,000 extradition's that were already processed. That is what I am talking about. Why would he do that? Maybe to appease his friends who put him where he is? I don't know why but he did. His actions are very wrong.

Again, let me say Obama did not start this problem. He had help from Mr. Clinton and George the Younger. Both were numbskulls when it came to immigration. But you see, the difference with President Obama, by his siding with Mexico and the rest of the world, he's opened our doors wide and said, "Come on in!" Why would he do that?

The first reason of course is why the Democrats have forever wanted illegal's to vote. It's simple math. If you can take care of the millions of illegals with welfare, health insurance and schools, they'll obviously vote for you. Why do you think they want the ballot box bilingual? That is a no brainer. That's Democratic politics at its best.

But our President sends smoke signals to the entire world that Mexico is the way to enter the United States? That is exactly what he did when he joined a lawsuit with Calderon. Our borders are now being crossed with traffic at the pace of rush hour on New York's George Washington Bridge.

The infiltration is no longer just poor, destitute Mexicans coming north for work and a better life. We're being flooded by terrorists, criminals and drug cartels. Where is Obama's grand dame of Homeland Security, Janet Napolitano on this issue? A very Interesting question.

Many would argue it is a humanitarian problem. To a great degree it is. Mexico has always had that problem. Mexico is also in the middle of a massive drug war that President Calderon blames on us, and Obama agrees with him. Obama does not like this country.

We have to consider there are also humanitarian problems in Bangladesh, India, Somalia, Darfur, and every Muslim nation in the world with the possible exception of Saudi Arabia. We aren't helping all of them by bringing them here?

There is something going on with the immigration problem from Mexico that is not right. It's not about the true immigrants that seek a better life. In America our foundation and our history is built on immigrants. I've lived several years in Texas, and the place would stop without immigrant workers. That is not the problem.

We built this country on immigrants--but not the immigrants we are getting today. The immigrants of old came to America to be part of what the country represented. They wanted to be part of the American dream and many helped build America and their own dreams.

My son-in-law is a great young man. We're blessed to have him in our family. He is of Mexican descent. His grandfather and his family came to this country as legal immigrants. They were proud of their families and their heritage. They also insisted everyone learn and speak English. They wanted to be part of America. His grandfather served four years in World War II in the glider corps. They are the immigrants who built America.

Look around you now. We are faced with immigrants who demand the right to fly their own flag, demand they be allowed to stop traffic and pray in the streets and wear a veil, masking their faces on their legally binding driver's license.

We are being infiltrated by an enemy who has a strong base camp in America. It is happening here and around the free world as we speak. It is time we wake up and realize our laws are being used against us. We've already had a Judge in Oklahoma overturn a vote of the people forbidding Sharia Law. How can that be? How can our President sit by and allow these actions to happen in America? He is the enemy in the White House. Those actions are pieces to his new puzzle for America.

We can watch other countries and see where we're headed. Germany got caught up in allowing immigrant families to bring their extended families, and it is running them financially into the ground.

In Canada, Courts recently ruled it is okay for a Muslim to receive welfare for all of his wives, not just the original. The man is claiming seven wives and getting paid for each, and no one in the 'family' works. Polygamy is not even legal there. And with Obama's hand on America's throttle we are racing to our downfall at warp speed.

There is a growing body of evidence that the drug cartels and the terrorists are joining forces. They're making deals among devils. They promote each other's objectives. And remember, these aren't Mother Teresa's choir boys we're talking about. They're very sophisticated. They employ the latest in weapons, surveillance and techniques. They mix the old with the new. On the one hand we discover 49 illegal Mexican immigrants inside the tank of a water truck. On the other hand the drug cartels new sophistication runs deep. They're known to use submersible watercraft that can travel undetected. They take drugs up our coastline. They use businesses on the U.S. side of the border to keep tabs on the whereabouts of our Border Patrol. They are a formidable foe.

They dig sophisticated tunnels. There is a growing body of evidence that suggests many of the so-called illegals are terrorists from the Middle East coming to the US through the systems of the drug cartels. It is here that we should be concerned about those 10,000 Stinger missiles missing from the 'youth revolution' in Libya. It all fits together.

We have a President who cozies up to the Mexican President who heads one of the most corrupt governments in the world. Our President blames our Governors for the problem of immigration.

All the while, the Mexican drug cartels are looking more and more like Islamic terrorists every single day. We see the use of professional killers, beheadings, car bombings and assassinations. All these nice folks live right on our border and own the human trafficking coming into this country. All the while our President is not concerned. Why would he do that?

We can no longer consider it a humanitarian issue; it is a risk to our national security. Talk to any border Governor. It is a massive problem. It could bankrupt our states. Who would benefit then? Think about that and decide.

In San Joaquin General Hospital in Stockton, California 70% of all births are 'anchor babies' of illegal immigrants. In 2010 Stockton School District was $25 million in the hole. The same statistic is true at Dallas General Hospital, 70% are 'anchor babies' of illegal immigrants.

The problem is not just financial. The Border Agents have their hands tied. They don't have a chance against the cartels. Their rules of engagement are only topped by the nonsensical rules of engagement our military men and women are held to in Afghanistan. Our politically correct world is killing us as our country is overrun by the enemy.

It's not just our PC world that's a problem on the border either. It's our Environmental Protection Agency too. Congress is working on passing a bill known as the Organ Mountains-Desert Peaks Wilderness Act. It would declare 25 miles of sparsely populated border area in New Mexico to be a 'wilderness preserve'.

Once they do that for the environmental lobby, the Border Patrol will be prevented from entering the border area. As one National Security Advisor said, "It's like a welcoming mat for the illegals". Why would a President allow his administration to do that?

While the Canadian border to the north is certainly less of a worry, the EPA is at work there too. There are wide areas of the Northwest where our Customs and Border Agents are not permitted to patrol because they are a path for grizzly bear migration back and forth across the border. Apparently the grizzlies are the only ones with free access on the northern border without a passport.

Our President continually makes a point of saying how secure our borders are, in spite of the evidence to the contrary. It doesn't seem to matter that our Governors say different. President Obama visited El Paso, Texas. He gave Governor Rick Perry the Netanyahu treatment by avoiding him. While there, he announced that America's borders are safer than ever. Why would he do that?

At the same time, as I mentioned earlier, Greta Van Susterin with Fox News was broadcasting live from south Texas, near the Mexican border. She was with Governor Perry. They were watching live footage of the infiltration freeway from Mexico into Texas. It was a grisly report of crimes and murder. In the report they noted the growing number of Middle Eastern types coming across the border. Yet our President says – we are safer than ever.

Why would a President do that? Obama was recently speaking to a Hispanic group in Washington regarding immigration and said, "I'd like to work my way around Congress". Soon after that speech the administration made a unilateral change in immigration law enforcement when it announced the government will no longer seek deportation of anyone other than those who have committed a 'series of crimes'.

The Washington Post asked in an editorial, "Only Congress has Constitutional authority to establish US immigration policy, and fundamental reform requires legislative action."

Thus the administration's recent announcement that deportations will be sought only for undocumented immigrants who have committed crimes in the United States violates the separation of powers and is unconstitutional." Did you hear that on the mainstream news?

Why does everyone see the problem except our President? Even France has tightened up immigration and recently banned the wearing of veils in public. The Dutch followed suit when Prime Minister Mark Rutte announced tougher rules for immigrants and asylum seekers wanting Dutch Nationality. If those seeking to move in are unable to show income they aren't welcome. Also, the wearing of veils was deemed not in keeping with a healthy public life.

Is our President really concerned about our homeland security? Would you know his concern by his actions? When highly respected former Marine General Jim Jones left the post of National Security Advisor, the President appointed one of his underlings to the top job. Tom Donilon is his name. The appointment was against the advice of General Jones, who said on a performance appraisal of Donilon, "He has never gone to Afghanistan or Iraq or really left the office for a serious business trip."

Defense Secretary Robert Gates reportedly told the President that Donilon "…would be a disaster as National Security Advisor, and that he did not understand the military or treat its senior leadership with sufficient respect."

After those rousing recommendations, Mr. Obama went ahead and named Donilon to the post. Our new National Security Advisor was incompetent before he started. And we wonder why our southern border leaks like a sieve?

- Does any of this bother you?

It really should. We may never know the root of Obama's disdain for America. We do know it runs deep by simply watching his actions. We must not worry about what he says, rather what he does. When you sue Governors, ignore Congress, change immigration laws, let the EPA put holes in our border – you do not have my county's interest at heart.

We have one more piece in the Obama puzzle. Flood the country with immigrants, turn a blind eye to the bad ones and increase our expenses to unaffordable levels. Reread those communist goals from 1960. Then read on …

"Communism has never come to power in a country that was not disrupted by war, corruption, or both."

President John F. Kennedy

*"A thorough knowledge of the Bible
is worth more than a college education."*

President Theodore Roosevelt

$15,000,000,000,000 and Counting

We passed that $15 trillion milestone as we speak. Most mortals can't relate to such a figure, let alone a debt of that amount. The 'Recovery Summer', as it was dubbed by the White House in 2010, sounds like a new summer blockbuster. But the 'Recovery Summer' I'm talking about is a horror movie starring none other than our President, Barack Hussein Obama and his supporting cast.

Our national debt is staggering in the least and alarming to most. Over half of our debt is owned by foreigners. Over one quarter of our debt is owned by the Chinese Communists alone. Does that sound like a great idea? A recent Office of Management and Budget (OMB) report states that the Chinese are in the process of a massive upgrade of their armed forces to challenge our dominance in the Pacific. We're funding that with our interest payments.

At a jobs council meeting in June of this year the President was called out, which we know he doesn't appreciate, for his comments on his stimulus projects not being quite as 'shovel ready' as he thought. As Gomer on Andy Griffith used to say, 'surprise, surprise'! The fact is, it was no surprise at all.

In an NBC interview the President said that one of the problems with the economic recovery was innovation and technology - like job stealing ATM's. That was one of the reasons why the employment rate was not rebounding as quickly as he hoped. He said ATM's are the problem.

I ask you everyday Americans, the uneducated masses like me, do you really think a degree from Occidental College, Columbia and Harvard Law School, are required to come up with a chicken shit response like that? The former Assistant Law Professor at the University of Chicago Law School thinks ATM's are a contributing factor to our unemployment? If that doesn't worry you; you're part of the problem.

In the news again are Fannie Mae and Freddie Mac. We just bailed these folks out a few months ago. They still owe the federal government millions of dollars. They are now before Congress trying to justify million-dollar bonuses for their top 10 executives. But the organization is still not making money. Where is our President on the issue? He is in Hawaii, on vacation and saying nothing.

I'm going to try something a little different as we discuss our Presidents economic policies. I guess it'll be a little like a subliminal message. Its a little update on whether we are better or worse since the Anointed One took office.

The Obama Administration said that by late June, 75% of its contract, grants and loans awarded through the stimulus package have been paid out. That means the government actually issued a check to those awarded money. Duh, what kind of measurement is that? You can pay the money to the awardees but no check and balance on what happened with it? Were jobs created? Where is the accountability for doing something with the money?

- **Change: Average price for a retail gallon of gas in January 2009 ... $1.83. The average in the summer of 2011 ... $3.44. That is a change of 84% for the worse.**

With the stimulus money that has been 'paid' out as a measurement, here is something to think about. What if US cities needing money, took the stimulus dollars, bought road equipment with the stimulus dollars and just parked it? Why would they do that? It seems if you park this new equipment for a spell, get with an auction company and auction it off for say 60 cents or so on the dollar ... you have 60% of the original stimulus money the government gave you with no strings attached. I think that's pretty clever. They can then use it for what they want.

For example take a look at what some other cities did with their homeland security stimulus dollars.

- El Reno, Oklahoma bought a decontamination trailer and a video security system for $55,000.

- The state of Nebraska spent $5,000 on scuba gear, $500,000 for fire training, $141,000 on a bomb robot and $17,000 on speakers for a helicopter.

- In Brigham City, Utah they spent $250,000 to retrofit a Senior Center.

- Boise, Idaho spent $1.8 million dollars on body bags, $3.4 million dollars on emergency vehicles and $41,000 securing an Albertsons distribution center.

- Buffalo, New York spent $935,000 on routine police patrols.

- The state of Georgia spent $100 million dollars to upgrade the emergency radio systems. It is now reported that communication is worse.

- In Garfield County Washington, officials spent $7,000 on an ATV and another $30,000 on an SUV.

- The State of Washington spent $343,000 on 30 bullet proof vests and an armored truck.

- The State of New Hampshire spent $116,000 dollars for radiation detection equipment for use at the Department of Motor Vehicles.

- Last, in Montgomery, Alabama they spent $150,000 to build a satellite imaging system for first responders. At its core is Google Earth, which is free to all of us.

You can't make this stuff up. The truth is too good. If the government required accountability and followed up they might know these things too. If there was accountability for spending and someone followed the stimulus dollars in some of Americas largest cities ... they might just find the exact buy and auction game I mentioned earlier. It is real.

- **Change: Average price of European crude (Brent barrel) in January of 2009 was $43.48. The average price in the summer of 2011 ... $99.02. That is a change of 127% for the worse.**

Mychal Massie is Chairman of the National Leadership Network of Black Conservatives. In an article he wrote entitled, '*When Will Obama Crack in Public?*' he says, "At a time when many Americans can barely afford Burger King and a movie, Obama boasts of spending a billion dollars on his re-election campaign". Think about that.

Questioned at a recent appearance about the spiraling fuel costs, Obama said, "Get used to it." With his patented Dennis the Menace grin he told another person at the event, who complained about the effect high fuel prices were having on his family, to "get a more fuel efficient car". Maybe the guy would, if he had a job?

- **Change: The average price of West Texas crude in January 2009 was $38.74. The average price in the summer of 2011 ... $91.38. That is a change of 136% for the worse.**

It's tough enough to have a President trashing our states like Arizona and Texas. But in these economic times it's harder to imagine that he's fighting South Carolina over the jobs Boeing wants to add by building a plant there? Ever thought that would happen in America? Not me.

His very public support of unions is another big piece to the Barackstar Puzzle. If you think back to the communist goals and his organizing training, you'll see clearly what I am talking about. Unions and revolts go back a long way and are all part of the plan.

President Obama turned majority share of General Motors over to their unions. The same unions who have made it impossible for GM to build a car cheap enough to compete. He also fired the President of GM and dictated salaries. Yet the same President has no comment on the bonuses of Fannie Mae and Freddie Mac executives? Remember, we watch actions, not words, to understand a person's real intent. Obama's is very clear.

- **Change: London Gold per Troy ounce in January 2009 was $853.25. The price when this analysis was done in the early part of summer 2011 was $1,369.50. An increase of 60.5%. Note: Late summer 2011, gold was in the $1,800 range.**

In September 2011, the President gave his latest economic speech. That's the one where he planned it on the same date as the pre-announced Republican Debate. His special guest for the speech was none other than Richard Trumka, President of the AFL/CIO. Mr. Trumka urged the President to 'go to the mat' for Big Labor. While details of his plan for yet another economic recovery are sketchy, the unions surely look to make big gains. Why not, with a President using the unions for votes and who knows what else down the road, they have to score big.

- **Change: Number 2 yellow corn in Central Illinois in January 2009 was $3.56 per bushel. The price in summer of 2011 was $6.33 per bushel. A mere 78.1% increase.**

President Trumka, the head of the AFL/CIO, brags that he is in the White House every week. Wonder why? Lots of union matters I guess. I guess they discuss matters like keeping Boeing's new plant from landing in South Carolina, a right-to-work state. Or, as I previously mentioned, they're busy aiming at the state of Texas, moving jobs from non-union Sealy, Texas to heavily unionized Wisconsin. That's important for a President to do while the country is in its worst economic condition since the Great Depression. Unions do not create jobs, businesses do.

- **Change: Number 1 yellow soybean in Central Illinois in January of 2009 was $9.66 per bushel. When this survey was completed in 2011 they were selling for $13.75 per bushel. Their price only jumped a modest 42.3% in the President's first two years in office.**

Trumka's been a thug since his days as President of the United Mineworkers Union. In the 1980's and 1990's, Trumka led three violent strikes in which militancy was involved. He actively encouraged it. For those who continued to work to provide for their families, there were threats and outright violence.

President Reagan took a different approach. He took on the Air Traffic Controllers and replaced them all. You didn't see him jumping into bed with any of the union presidents. He acted for the good of the nation, not himself. Our man in the White House now is no Reagan.

Does the Presidents allegiance to unions stop with Trumka? No. Teamsters Union President Jimmy Hoffa, not the one under the Meadowlands, but his son, is buddies with Trumka, and the President. They are three peas in a pod of disgust.

- **Change: Raw sugar cane FOB in January 2009 was $13.37. Two years later is was $35.39. An unbelievable increase of 164.7%.**

On Labor Day, 2011, President Obama shared the podium with none other than Richard Trumka and Jimmy Hoffa the Younger. Both are militants and heads of large unions. True to form and just like his father, Jimmy let loose with a foul mouthed barrage reminiscent of the old days when my Dad was negotiating national contracts with Jimmy's now deceased Father at the Palmer House in downtown Chicago.

Jimmy Hoffa the Younger said, while introducing our great President on Labor Day, urging his union militants to 'take out those sons of bitches'. Jimmy was referring to the 49% of us who disagreed and did not support the election of Barack Hussein Obama. Isn't that interesting?

- **Change: Unemployment rate non-farm overall in January 2009 was 7.6%. At the time of this survey two years later it was 9.4%. That's an increase of only 23.7% but it's still a whole bunch of people.**

Does anyone listen to these union thugs anymore? You'd think not, with our enlightened 21st century bells and whistles and all that fancy education and save the planet stuff. But we're not beyond it, and thanks to our President, it's now a growth industry.

The Associated Press reported shortly after the Labor Day speech that hundreds of Longshoreman in Longview, Washington took several security guards hostage for hours at the port there. Nice folks I'm sure. The militant longshoreman reportedly committed various acts of vandalism and violence.

They broke windows, cut brake lines on railroad cars and threatened police officers with baseball bats. Wow! Sounds more like a prison riot. The local Police Chief told AP that the union militants told him 'this is only the start'. The Police Chief made no arrests. He must believe in the old pickup basketball rule, 'no harm, no foul'?

- **Change: Unemployment rate - Blacks in January 2009 was 12.6%. Two years later it was 15.8%. That's an increase of 25.4%, which is slightly worse than Unemployment for all non-farms. I haven't checked into it but it's probably George the Younger's fault.**

It must have steamed this trio of malcontents when Governor Scott Walker of Wisconsin took his stand on the states unions. Remember the protests in the streets of Madison, the shutting down of offices and the bussing in of reinforcements? It's the union way. They're now leading a recall election of the Governor. Wisconsin Senate Democratic leader Mark Miller cried out like a frightened puppy. He said, "This is a disaster!" Miller, union officials and protesters, all predicted catastrophe.

The state was taken to court and somehow prevailed. They must have really been lucky to draw a conservative judge in Wisconsin. The funny thing is that disaster didn't happen. The state of the state is much improved.

Our future as America depends on more Scott Walkers. We need one in the White House. The early returns for Wisconsin are very positive. Yes, they're early, but it is a small indication of what's possible.

The Kaukauna School District in the Fox River Valley near Appleton is the first winner. They were about to close. The good news is the district did not have to close. It had been running a $400,000 deficit. Money it didn't have. After Governor Walker's changes the school will have a surplus of $1.5 million dollars. The changes are working for Wisconsin. That is the leadership we need in Washington.

- **Change: Number of unemployed in January 2009 was 11,616,000. Two years later the unemployment number was 14,485,000. An increase of 24.7%. In human terms, for you bureaucrats, that means real people.**

  The number of people unemployed increased in the past two years by 2,869,000 people. That means human beings, with families. Imagine if you live in Iowa. Our unemployment numbers are equal to the entire population of Iowa being out of work. Think about that one. Yet, Emperor Barack says, 'just go buy an energy efficient car'.

The changes made in Wisconsin were straightforward. Previously, employees paid 10% of their health care costs and 0% of their pension. Today they pay 12.6% of their healthcare and 5.8% of their pensions. Seems only right, the private sector pays far more, especially for pensions, if they even have one.

The other change, not considered in the $1.5 million surplus projection, is the right to negotiate their healthcare with others besides the WTA, an insurance organization created by the Wisconsin teachers union. In the past, it was pay the piper and the piper was the union. Now they can level the playing field and negotiate with many companies for their benefits.

I remember my days with Frito Lay. In the 80's we decertified a number of Teamsters Unions around the United States. What was the biggest savings? It was to provide all employee benefits through Frito and not through the Teamsters. The savings were massive and the coverage better. It was a no brainer.

In the case of the Kaukauna School District the savings didn't stop there. When there was no longer a collective bargaining agreement, they went out for bids for the insurance and pension. The Wisconsin Teachers Association (WTA) suddenly says, "We can match the lowest bid". I wouldn't have given them the business because they've been lying to me for years. The school district did allow them to bid and keep the insurance, for now. The cost cuts were dramatic, and they'd been overpaying for years just like Frito Lay.

Another savings came in hours worked. The old collective bargaining agreement stipulated that the teachers work only 37.5 hours per week and teach no more than 5 out of 7 periods a day. They now work 40 hours per week like most Americans if they're lucky, and teach 6 periods a day out of 7. These changes enabled the District to reduce high school class size from 31 students per class to 26 and for elementary classes they were reduced from 26 to 23. What is wrong with that?

Teacher salaries remain the same, with the exception of the money they now pay towards their own benefits. The highest salary for a teacher in the District is $80,000 per year plus the cost of $35,000 for benefits, which the employees pay a percentage of. The pay and benefits is for a 184 day work year with summers off. I'll bet some of those unemployed in America would love a chance at one of these jobs.

- **Change: Number of Federal employees as of January 2009 was 2,779,000. After two years the number is 2,840,000. The change is a growth of 2.2% or 69,000 people. That number is much greater today and we'll cover that later.**

  We do know is that the private sector lost 2,869,000 jobs and the government gained 69,000 jobs? Tell me in what world is that okay? I don't know, I think a socialist one?

Let's check out the new 'Green World' the President is cramming down our throats. Of course it doesn't include his buddy and former Green Jobs Czar, Van Jones, who has since resigned.

In May of 2010 President Obama stood in the California factory of Solyndra LLC and said, "The promise of clean energy isn't just an article of faith." He was standing before the workers who were making solar-power panels that were subsidized by our taxes. What a deal!

What wasn't carefully noted, well, not noted at all, was that two months prior to the President's visit, Price Waterhouse accounting firm warned that Solyndra, the recipient of $535 million in Federal loan guarantees had some financial problems, raising significant doubt about its ability to repay any loans.

Obama ignored the Price Waterhouse warning and supported Solyndra. The company then cancelled a planned public stock offering. Then they failed in an attempt to get refinancing. Then a deal was cut to bring in new investors. The new investors were good to go, as long as they came before government money in the case of default. That is a violation of federal law.

The fairy tale Obama started, ended on September 6, 2011, when Solyndra filed for bankruptcy protection. On September 8, 2011, the FBI raided Solyndra's Headquarters. Jonathan Dorsheimer, an analyst for Canaccord Genuity Inc. of Vancouver, said in an interview, "People, including our government, put blinders on and did not want to believe the obvious. The fact that the government chose Solyndra as their white horse is mind-boggling".

Air Force General William Shelton was urged by the White House to change his testimony before Congress to make it more favorable for Solyndra. To his credit the four star General didn't do it.

Since the news broke, Congress is investigating, and emails have surfaced showing folks in the White House were asking Solyndra executives to delay the announcement of their bankruptcy until after the fall elections. Sure makes us feel good about our new change in the White House doesn't it?

White House spokesman Eric Schultz, responded in an email statement, "Selection of companies to receive US backing are merit-based decisions made by career staffers at the Department of Energy, and the process for this particular loan guarantee began under George W. Bush." There he is, Bush the Younger causing trouble again. They must have a cardboard cutout of that man in the Oval Office they throw darts at?

The program under which Solyndra got funding was authorized by Congress in 2005. Yep, George the Younger was President then. During the Bush administration, Solyndra was identified but not acted upon. Does that make Bush the Younger responsible?

Under the current administration, Energy Secretary Steven Chu pledged during his Senate confirmation hearing that he would 'speed up' the approval applications, and apparently he did.

Solyndra was given conditional approval in March 2009, with final approval in September. Isn't that clever how the White House spokesperson blamed that on George the Younger? My Dad always said, "Read the fine print Ed, read the fine print."

"We smelled a rat at the onset!" said Fred Upton a Michigan Representative and Cliff Stearns a Representative from Florida. Both head some long named committees and sub-committees in Congress. Apparently the stench of that rat wasn't quite strong enough to make them act quickly. They made these strong statements the day the company announced it had laid off its entire workforce of 1,100 human beings. And think about it, how many solar panels do you have to sell to support 1,100 people?

- **Change: Real median household income was $50,112 in January of 2009. Two years later it was $49,777. A dip of only .007%. Remember, that number is for those people still working.**

When you cut through all the solar panels sitting in the warehouse at Solyndra, the project was a big green failure. What Obama apparently missed at Columbia and Harvard is that products need a market. It's the same with his green cars and everything else. You can't push products on a market if they don't want them. That is Business 101.

You're going to hear lots more about Solyndra, probably only on Fox News; the story isn't finished yet. Early news from the investigations indicates there is a connection between Solyndra and a billionaire by the name of George Kaiser.

Mr. Kaiser is an Obama Campaign fundraiser. The George Kaiser Family Foundation, a 'charitable' organization based in Tulsa holds about 36.7% of the Solyndra Company. Interesting? As the plot thickens we find California Representative Henry Waxman and Diana DeGette a Colorado Representative saying two months ago, "The Company is in a strong financial position." Think 'Fannie Mae and Freddie Mac and Barney Frank' ... oh, on second thought, don't think about the disgusting Barney Frank.

The CEO of Solyndra tells Congress they should 'separate Solyndra and its business results from the political process.' And I'll bet he does want them to do that, as he relaxes in bed at home and thinks of the Enron crowd in cell block 6.

Mr. Kaiser paid the White House and the President's Aides 16 visits since 2009. Of course but he swears he didn't inhale or have sex with any of them. An emailed statement from the George Kaiser Family Foundation on September 1 this year said, "George Kaiser is not an investor in Solyndra and did not participate in any discussions with the US government regarding the loan." I'm sure Mr. Kaiser has nothing to do with the organization that bears his name, nothing at all.

For those of you who believe that one, we have some land in Florida leftover from the 60's. It's the land sale the Teamsters made to their members. It turned out to be swamp land from Jimmy the Older, but hey, it's warm down there most of the year. I think the Solyndra deal is down in the swamp as well. Look for it on 48 Hours, after the break.

- **Change: Number of Food Stamp Recipients as of January 2009 was 31,983,716 people. Two years later it was 43,200,878 people. An increase of 35.1%! That's a difference of a mere 11,217,162 people.**

The increase is like adding the entire population of New York City to the welfare rolls since Barry took office. Of course we don't know how many of those poor folks are illegal immigrants granted the privilege of our tax dollars, either.

The First Couple is certainly a real rags-to-riches story. He goes from poor boy in Hawaii, to college to Community Organizer to State Senator and on to the Presidency like he was shot from a cannon. It's an amazing story?

His wife Michelle gets a job at the University of Chicago Medical Center for $120,000 a year. Her job was to run programs for community relations, neighborhood outreach, volunteer recruitment, staff diversity and minority contracting. That sounds right up her alley from the things she learned from hubby Barack on the mean streets of Chicago.

While Michelle worked her fingers off at the University Medical Center, husband Barack turns on the afterburners and leaps from the Illinois Senate right into the US Senate. Immediately after that miraculous achievement, wife Michelle receives a raise. It wasn't a raise like you and I get, it was the mother of all raises. Her salary was increased to $317,000 a year! She must have done some damned good recruitment of volunteers or really, I mean really, reached out to the neighborhood. That is an increase of $197,000 a year! You do the math on how big that increase is? I can't.

Don't you wish the story ended there? One big coincidence you say? Don't you wish you knew their secret of success? It could be mere coincidence. It seems to follow the First Couple. When Senator Barack Obama was appointed to his new position; he requested an 'earmark' in legislation for $1,000,000 to the University of Chicago Medical Center. Coincidence must be our First Couples middle name. No, that's right, his is Hussein.

First lady Michelle, as we said earlier, is proud of America for the first time in her life. She should be! She leaves her job to become our Firstest Lady in the White House. The UC Medical Center back in Chicago said in a public statement that her position will remain unfilled. As a friend of mine from Holland said when he first saw homes in America ... UNBEEEEELIEVVV ... ABLE! She must have gotten everything organized before she left?

- **Change: Number of Long Term Unemployed in January 2009 was 2,600,000. Two years later it is 6,400,000 people. That's an increase of 146.2%. I don't know how long is long, but I do know, that statistic is a painful one for many Americans.**

Since taking office President Obama has achieved one thing no President before him has achieved. The 100 year AAA credit rating of the United States of America has survived World War I, The Great Flu Epidemic, Warren G. Harding, Prohibition, The 1929 Stock Market Crash, The Great Depression, FDR, World War II, The Atomic Bomb, My Birth, The Korean War, The Vietnam War, The Kennedy Assassination, Lyndon Johnson, Richard Nixon, Jimmy Carter, George W. Bush, 9-11, but two years of the Obama administration and we're downgraded.

Okay, it took other Presidents to get us here and awful people in Congress too. They all steered the car and drove it towards the cliff. I get that. My problem with Mr. Obama is, when he took over the wheel of the car called America, he hit the spending peddle like a 14 year old stealing a Maserati. He hasn't let up yet. He's smoking the tires off. The RPM's are maxing out and we're either going off the cliff or hitting a rock wall. Take your choice or change drivers.

- **Change: Poverty Rate for Individuals in January 2009 was 13.2%. Two years later it was 14.3%. An increase of 8.3%. That can't be good.**

I wrote much of this book at my cottage in Canada this summer. The one I no longer own. I love reading newspapers as I travel. In a recent Sudbury Star there was an interesting article from one of their writers Ezra Levant entitled, *Obama Must Stop Blaming and Spending*. It's good to get another perspective.

I'll just share a few of the points the article made. He begins with, "Did you really understand that debt ceiling debate that dominated Washington this past month? We had very stern speeches by both the Republicans and Democrats. US President Barack Obama gave what felt like the 700th speech of his Presidency. But there's a bit of a difference between knowing how to read a teleprompter and knowing how to run a country."

Let's stop right there. Fox News didn't say that. It came from a small town editorial in the near north of Ontario, a country and world away from Washington. I spent about three months there this summer. I was often asked, "What is wrong with you people?" They would then explain they didn't mean the American people but American politicians.

One night a Brit stopped over to our cottage for a chat. He now lives in Canada. He said, "Ed, what is happening to America? Your blokes in politics have lost their minds".

Mr. Levant of the Sudbury Star went on in his article, "Unemployment is now 9.1% in the US - two points higher than in Canada. Their banks continue to fail. Consumer confidence is low. It's a double-dip recession - a second recession happening right after the first. But it's not just unemployment and slow economic growth.

It's insane spending by government. From bank bailouts to Car Company bailouts to union bailouts to nationalizing health care, there's nothing Obama won't throw money at. Trouble is he doesn't have the money - so he's borrowing it at a rate unprecedented in human history."

Mr. Levant called our Presidents spending, 'unprecedented in human history'. His editorial is dated August 9, 2011. He lives 1000 miles north of our Capital. He sees it, and many of us don't. We must wake up, and wake up now. We are losing our country! The spending is part of a plan to bring us down like Reagan brought down the Soviet Union.

Mr. Levant points out that we go to China for more money and high five around Capitol Hill on our $2 trillion dollars we've added to our already outlandish, at that time $14 trillion debt. He likens it to a husband and wife ecstatic over agreeing to accept a higher line of credit on their cards when they're already broke. Do you see how truly crazy this is?

Mr. Levant is writing after our credit rating was downgraded by Standard &Poor. He notes that the following Monday, Moody's was considering the same. But what did Obama and the Democrats do? Mr. Levant's words not mine, "Obama's party, the Democrats, have gone into full blame storming mode".

He was referring to a few comments from the Dem's. John Kerry said, "The credit downgrade is the fault of the Tea Party anti-spending movement." Then there's the always lovable Barney Frank who said, "It was because of the US Military." Way to nail it Barney, just like you did the junk mortgage meltdown in 2008. Levant closes with, "Obama's White House, never too good with math - said, "The S&P got their math wrong." I'm sure they did Barry, I'm sure they did.

Isn't it amazing that none of this has been observed or reported by the mainstream media in the United States? Well, Fox does report it, but who else does? His editorial further reads, "It says a lot about Obama that he is outraged at the messenger. Sort of like being woken up by a fire alarm and being mad about the noise and not the fire."

It's a great observation and analogy. We're on fire folks! Our President would rather go after his dissenters than put out the fire. He just throws more flaming darts at his George the Younger cutout.

Mr. Levant ends his editorial with this note, referring to the reality we face financially, "It took outside observers to do it. America, the world's great engine of freedom and prosperity, the world's guarantor of security for 60 years, and the moral beacon to billions - has been weakened." He goes on to write, "Is Obama upset about this debt downgrade? Yes, because it could interfere with his plans for re-election. But he's not upset with the real problem: The beggaring of America and suffocation of its entrepreneurial spirit".

That's a pretty sad commentary from our good neighbor to the north. It's not from Hannity, or Rush, or any of the other pundits the liberals love to hate. It's not the dammed Republicans; it's from a wise young man in Canada.

- **Change: The number of people in poverty in the US in January of 2009 was 39,800,000. Two years later it is 43,600,000. An increase of 9.5% in two years, mind you. That is very sad in the greatest nation on earth that an additional 9,800,000 human beings fell below the poverty line since the Obama took office.**

Let's shift to a topic near and dear to American's hearts, gas prices. Obama decided in June 2011 to release 30 million barrels of oil from our Strategic Petroleum Reserve.

Do we have a national emergency? The Reserve is a national security inventory used to protect America from 'severe energy supply disruption'. To release petroleum from our strategic reserve requires meeting three conditions:

- An emergency situation exists and there is a significant reduction in supply which is of significant scope and duration;

- A severe increase in the price of petroleum products has resulted from such emergency situation; and

- Such price increase is likely to cause a major adverse impact on the national economy.

Do you think those three conditions were met? Hardly! When President Obama announced his decision to release those 30,000,000 barrels, he said it was because of the war in Libya and the supply disruption. What he failed to mention was that the majority of Libyan production goes straight to Europe, not the United States.

The following day, White House mouthpiece Jay Carney told reporters, "it was meant as protection against increasing gas prices over the summer driving season." If Carney is right, the move was for summer but nearly too late in late June. Either way, the two statements conflict, making one of them false. So what is Obama up to with this one?

The Washington Post's entire Editorial Board wrote a scathing editorial entitled, 'The Wrong Reason for Depleting the Strategic Oil Reserve.' They argued that it is more likely a 'political emergency' rather than the real one which is required. I believe it's a political ploy for some PR points with the motorists who are also voters?

To put the President's decision in perspective, the entire global market uses 84 million barrels of oil a day. Obama's actions would supply 1 million barrels of that for 30 days. Think about that and why he released the oil?

The release was actually part of an agreement Obama made with the International Energy Agency to release 60,000,000 barrels into the 'market' in the 30 days following the decision. The deal meant America would cough up 30 million barrels and 27 other countries would make up the other 30 million barrels. It was an international deal. Surprised?

Once again, Emperor Barack makes a deal with the 'international' community he loves. In his mind we already have a one-world government. It's all global now, including his ambitions and plans for America.

- **Change: Number of unemployment benefit recipients in January 2009 was 7,526,598. Two years later it was 9,193,838. An increase of 22.2%. For those new 1,667,240 people, living, breathing human beings ... they've probably had enough change for awhile.**

After announcing yet another job-building stimulus package, Obama is on the campaign trail now, using taxpayer dollars as a way to push his economic plans.

While in North Carolina stumping for reelection, one of his many raving fans yelled, "I love you!" Back in the campaign mode, Barry yelled his standard answer, "I love you back!" He then added a clever new one, "If you love me, you got to help me pass this bill!" Referring of course to the latest $447 billion he wants to spend. The crowds cheered. Will love win? I hope not.

We all remember Anthony Weiner, a Democratic Congressman and first class creep and pervert from New York. With Anthony gone from Congress a special election was held to replace him. A Republican by the name of Bob Turner pulled the upset of the century. He's the first Republican to hold the seat from that New York district since 1923. It was apropos when Donald Trump, a New Yorker, released a statement saying, *"Obama just doesn't get it."*

The Donald is no wall flower, certainly, and he minced no words on the subject. In the first half of his press release, he talks about the surprise of a Republican winning that particular House District. It also happens to be in the district where he grew up. He says his father was probably the only Republican who lived there. Trump explains his rationale as to why it happened and discussed the attributes of the newly elected Mr. Turner. Then he got plain and simple about what's wrong with our President, Obama.

The Donald says, "It goes without saying that Obama will not get the message. In fact, he will continue to double down on his anti-property policies. Only this past Monday did he release yet another plan under the guise of a 'jobs bill' which promises to raise taxes on those who actually hire workers and have capital. He just doesn't get it." Amen to that brother!

In all we've discussed, one thing is clear. Obama wants a bigger government. He also wants a government that takes care of you from cradle to grave. He is a man who has never created one job in his life. He has never managed a budget, let alone a country. He doesn't understand folks who create jobs, our entrepreneurs. Or, he doesn't care. The truth is that he has no interest. The darker truth is that he is President of a country he doesn't like and is working hard to change.

The change he was talking about was a change to something he and Michelle, Bill Ayers, Cass Sunstein, Hugo Chavez and George Soros to name a few, would like to see. It's a change to Socialism. It's killing the America we know. The America represents the freedom mankind enjoys today.

- **Change: US Rank in Economic Freedom World Rankings in January 2009 was number 5. Two years later we are ranked by the same index at number 9.**

  Not really a good direction to be traveling for a once great nation at the top. With Obama's hand on the throttle, we are racing towards destruction of our democratic way of life. It's all part of the plan.

The President doesn't get it. He's back on the campaign trail, visiting only battleground political states of course, still selling his latest stimulus package. The President says the House can pass all or parts of the legislation. That is designed to make him look good and Congress not so much.

At the same time, yet, one of his closest Advisors, David Axelrod, said, "The President has a package, the package works together. We need to do many things to get this economy moving." The next day, speaking to a group of Hispanics, the President said, "Obviously, if Congress passes parts of it, I'm not going to veto those parts." Which is it? Seems like some more double talk to me?

Axelrod told George Stephanopoulos that, "We're not in a negotiation to break up the package. It's not an a la carte menu. It's a strategy to get this country going." The President says, "I will sign it, but I will say then 'give me the rest'. I will keep on making that argument as long as the need is there to put people back to work". Could it be that Axelrod and Obama are saying the same thing? It's really hard to tell.

White House economic advisor Gene Sperling told reporters that the administration will make a 'strong' push for Congress to pass the plan all at once, but said that if it is approved piecemeal, the White House would work to persuade Congress to pass the remaining parts. It sounds to me like a conversation between the Smother Brothers.

What's really happening is very clever politics. Obama goes on the road telling voters 'personally' that he is easy to work with and Congress can do just about anything they want with his new bill. If we read between the double speak, he is more interested in setting up Congress as the fall guys. He speaks out of both sides of his mouth and will do anything to get his way.

- **Change: The National Debt in January 2009 was $10,000,000,000,000 (that's trillions). Two years of Obama and his high spending habits, it's now $15,000,000,000,000. A hefty little increase of 50.0% in a mere two years. What's a few 0's among us friends.**

Will President Obama ever 'get it' as the Donald asks? The problem is what 'he' gets isn't what we 'get'. Any normal American, who found themselves in the proverbial hole financially he claims Bush the Younger left him, would stop digging. Why does Obama, with a shovel in each hand, dig faster and faster? He must have learned the first rule of holes at Harvard, stop digging. No, Obama wants us to go down financially; the move to socialism is that much easier.

If we purely watch the Presidents words we'd see he will say anything. In a June 2008, in St. Paul, Minnesota, our President actually said in a speech that he would make the ocean waters recede. It's true. It was in reference to the impact of his green initiatives on the global climate.

He can make the oceans recede but he can't get a handle on the federal budget. The number of Federal bureaucrats making over $100,000 a year has gone from 14% to 19%. Times are tough for you but not the government. In the year after Obama's last stimulus package, the private sector lost 2,500,000 jobs while the government added over 400,000. That is a real problem.

In the deepest bowels of the first downturn the Department of Transportation had just one employee earning over $170,000 per year. Two years later it has 1,600. It's really tough fighting those terrorists stateside.

We find that the Federal Reserve slips the banking industry a cool $7.7 million in funds, funds the government printed, to help with the recovery. Congress was not consulted nor did they know until recently. The banks interest rate from the government … .001%. The rate the banks loaned money back to the government … .03%. That's brilliant and illegal!

We're completely out of control, and only the pilot of our craft is heading us straight into socialist arms. I'm more convinced than ever we do not know our President's real background. The Weekly Standard's Stephen Hayes wrote, "In his world everything is political and everything is about appearances." Can you see that now? Does it bother you?

Obama was voted in by 51% of Americans. We voted him in with no experience and a protected background. His educational experience is unverified, his campaign financing is questionable and his rise to stardom was quick and easy. He has less private sector business experience in his Cabinet than any administration going back at least a century. How could we have let this happen?

We as Americans, have to accept the fact that Obama is a self-inflicted wound. America voted the man into office.

It doesn't matter why you might have supported him, it only matters that you realize we must correct the mistake this election, or we'll all be living a change we didn't bargain for. We must fix it before it is too late, and it may be too late already.

In 2009, Reuters reported, "Washington DC has become the favorite area for wealthy young adults, with the nation's highest percentage of 25-34 year olds making more than $100,000 a year." Newsweek reported that of the top ten wealthiest counties in the United States, the majority surrounded the nation's capital. In all government categories combined, they devour 40 cents of every dollar American workers generate. That figure will rise, since fewer American workers are generating anything.

Government has become a big business. Senators and Congressmen go to Washington and become rich. They stay forever. They pay back their constituents with pork barrel spending. They become lobbyists and support lobbyists. It has to stop now!

What many Americans don't realize is that the government produces nothing. It is a consumer, it spends. Its only revenue is our taxes. You must realize that government employ's 16% of everyone in America. If you add the 8% of the people on government assistance that is 24% of Americans with a real need to vote for a bigger government. That isn't counting the spouses. That is ass backwards.

We have more education in America but we're getting dumber about what really matters.

- **Change: We must change. We must change now. We must vote this Marxist out in the 2012 election!**

The time is now. We're being economically destroyed as part of a plan by our President and those unknowns who support him. I'm not in a position to know exactly 'who' his supporters really are, other than what I shared. What I do know, when I read the communist goals, is that they have been and are being achieved right now. Our economy going down is part of that plan. And our Commander in Chief has other plans for the military as well.

"Carry the battle to them. Don't let them bring it to you. Put them on the defensive and don't ever apologize for anything."

President Harry S. Truman

"Look, it's an all volunteer force. Nobody made these guys go to war. They had to have known and accepted the risks. Now they whine about bearing the costs of their choice? It doesn't compute ... I thought these were people who were proud to sacrifice for their country? I wasn't asking for blood, just money. With the country facing the worst financial crisis in its history, I'd have thought that the patriotic thing to do would be to try to help reduce the nation's deficit. I guess I underestimated the selfishness of some of my fellow Americans."

President Barack Hussein Obama
(After cancelling his plan to enact military pay cuts first during the supposed government shutdown in 2011)

"How do you tell a communist? Well, it's someone who reads Marx and Lenin. And how do you tell an anti-Communist? It's someone who understands Marx and Lenin."

President Ronald Reagan

Obama, Our Commander in Chief

Our military's supreme commander begins a Veterans Day service welcoming everyone to Memorial Day. Do you suppose he is that stupid, or he does this intentionally? This is a very difficult chapter for me. As a Marine who fought in Nam, I love America. I'm proud to have served my country along with the millions before and after me. But the man with all the supposed degrees from Occidental, Columbia and Harvard couldn't even pronounce the name of my beloved United States Marine Corps. He called it the United States Marine 'Corpse'. For me, that was too much to overcome.

He apparently didn't learn from his previous blunder. He recently referred to a Navy Corpsman as a Navy 'Corpseman'. I can only wonder if his statements are contentious or ignorant. But you know what? Not a word in the mainstream media, not even a mention. If that had been George the Younger the media would have had a circus. But Teflon Barry got a pass. He remains the media darling, even if he went to Harvard and can't pronounce Corps right.

Our new Commander skipped the Medal of Honor Ball during the Inauguration. I'm not a mental genius but that was a clue. If you're our country's head of the military, wouldn't you make it a priority, with two wars going on; to stop by for just a few minutes to pay tribute to the highest honored men in uniform? What this guy didn't know, care about or understand, was that for thousands of veterans around the country, his actions are a big red flag.

I learned in the Marine Corps in Parris Island that we should love God, Country and Corps in that order. I grew up in a small Ohio town around a lot of World War II vets who loved their country, too. That makes this guy very tough for me to accept as our Commander in Chief.

I've always felt, with the world the way it is and always has been, we need a Commander in Chief who the rest of the world is a wee bit wary of. Think about it. When Richard Nixon, Ronald Reagan or even Bush the Older was President, the crazies in the world weren't out there pulling stunts. When Jimmy Carter, Bill Clinton and now Mr. Obama is President, the world community does whatever it wants to us.

President Truman proved his grit, as did Eisenhower. Kennedy stared down the Russians during the Cuban Missile Crisis. President Carter did one thing that was very important. He brokered the mid-East peace deal between Israel, Jordan and Egypt. That was and is big. Obama tossed that out of the window with the Arab Spring. He's been kissing up to the entire world that's against us with no results. I wonder why?

I'm in my sixth decade and counting on this earth. I've traveled to 19 or 20 countries. I still love America, faults and all. In all that time I never referred to a President as anything other than Mr. President. I hate to say it but that is not the case with President Obama. It's very difficult to call him President, but I try. It is more difficult to see him as our Commander in Chief. But as Americans, we have no one to blame but ourselves. We voted him in with 51% of the vote.

Nonetheless, he's now the Commander in Chief of our military throughout the world. If you are China or Russia, are you thinking twice about America's might? He wants to make America a demilitarized zone. Left to his own devices, he will make our military the smallest it has ever been. Believe it!

To be a Commander in Chief you must provide leadership. How do you think our men and women in the military feel about his leadership considering a few of his actions listed below?

- The President's World Apology Tour

- He places a new commander in Afghanistan and drags his feet for three months before replying to his request for more troops.

- When he answers he denies the request and provides him with a reduced troop count.

- The President is seen bowing to the King of Saudi Arabia.

- The President is seen praying during Ramadan.

- The President visits Japan, bows to the Emperor and attempts to apologize for dropping the big one in World War II.

- The President cannot pronounce the name of the United States Marine Corps or their partners, Navy Corpsmen.

- He decided, during a budget crunch, that if his budget isn't passed, the military payroll will be the first expense to stop. All this while we have troops fighting on two fronts.

- He replaces his first commander in Afghanistan with General Stanley McCrystal. A special operations warrior and a man loved by the troops. He then fires him for his and his subordinates speaking out in Rolling Stone magazine.

- His major priority is implementing a new gays in the military policy against the military's recommendation and while we have troops in two theaters of war.

As part of the President's new gays in the military policy, the Pentagon issued orders to all Chaplains to perform same-sex marriages. In response the Catholic Church informed the military that Catholic Chaplains would not be performing same-sex marriages. The Chaplain Alliance for Religious Liberty followed suit with a similar statement. They represent over 2,000 Chaplains. Is that a fight you want in the middle of a war?

Why would a President do any of this? You really need to think hard about how his actions made our servicemen and women feel. Especially those serving in combat areas. I can tell you how it felt in Vietnam when Jane Fonda showed up in Hanoi sitting in a gun turret with North Vietnamese soldiers. It was disgusting! We had no respect for President Johnson when he let her get away with her treasonous acts. To this day none of her movies have ever been shown in my home, and I liked her as an actress.

The lies of President Johnson and Secretary of Defense Robert McNamara took a toll. We may have been young, but we weren't stupid. Back then we didn't have text messaging or email, but we did read newspapers. What your leader says, does impact your attitude. It did then and it does even more so right now.

When you're fighting a war you need to know your Commander in Chief is in it with you. I believe President Johnson's heart was with us. But he gave way to the ways of Washington and eventually sold us out. Our Marine Commanders were not part of that problem. One man stands out, Colonel Masterpool. He was a real leader.

We were once in a battle near the DMZ, near North Vietnam. He was our Commander. At the end of the battle we were to return to our base at Dong Ha, South Vietnam. It was 10, maybe 12 miles to our east. Our choppers did not arrive. We were tired, hungry and beat after three weeks of fighting in the jungle of the DMZ.

Colonel Masterpool told us he would march us home, at night, and when we arrived we would have steaks. A chopper arrived to pick up the walking wounded. All refused the ride and walked with Colonel Masterpool. It wasn't easy but we would have followed him to hell and back. He was with us every step of the way. He was our leader. We need that kind of leader today. We do not have that man in the White House. Our Commander in Chief displays his disdain for the military every single day and it makes following him very difficult.

Today's military is very intelligent. They are the best educated men and women we have ever put in uniform. They aren't the dummy draftees the Vietnam Vet's were made to look like. We have a professional military that deserves to be led by a professional leader. Mr. Obama is not that leader.

President Obama has made overtures to our enemies many times over. Wouldn't it be nice if we could trust all those folks who have lied to us over the past few decades? What a great world it would be if that were to really happen. I'd join in the celebration. But history shows it is not the case.

Do you think Pakistan can be trusted? How about Imanutjob in Iran? We know we can count on North Korea for sure? China? Russia? Come on. When we cut our military back like Obama wants do and lead in a politically correct way, what does that say to the our troops? Do you think they feel secure? Those are the people risking their lives for America.

How do you think the troops feel when they're at war and their Commander sneaks out to hit a few golf balls on our most somber day of the year, Memorial Day? It was also the day North Korea test fired their first nuke. Is that leadership? Is that showing respect for the thousands upon thousands of Americans who died defending this President's right to live the American Dream? You should be angry by now, and I pray it drives you to action.

We have a President who spends his time filling out March Madness brackets and appearing on Jay Leno or David Letterman. He parades around the White House with his shirt off, sometimes with his hat on backwards; looking more like a rapper come to Washington than our Commander in Chief.

You think our troops don't know about his disrespect of the office? They do! He is pictured all the time with his feet up in the Oval Office, where great men have preceded him and respected the office they held. Leaders show respect and give it. He does not.

What about the gift he presented the Queen of England. He gave Her Majesty an iPod, with recordings of his speeches on it! She gave him a rare book. She already had an iPod, like many people in the free world. Of course he gave Prime Minister Gordon Brown, a set of DVD's that weren't formatted for British use. That's leadership? It may just all be by design to put down our allies.

If you think his behavior doesn't impact our troops, think again. A decorated career Marine I know who served in Iraq, the Battles for Fallujah and Afghanistan called me this week. We were discussing his career and his thoughts of getting out after over a decade in the Corps. He said it had nothing to do with the Marine Corps that he loves. It had everything to do with our leadership, our Commander in Chief and Congress.

He said it started back when Congress and the White House were full of drama over the government being shutdown because no budget had been passed. The White House came out with their list of who wasn't getting paid first, 'if' they didn't pass the budget deal. The list included the US military and their retirees right on top.

Think about that. Our young men and women are fighting in Afghanistan and exposed in Iraq, and the Commander in Chief won't pay them first. What kind of message is that to our young folks fighting a war? Obama either doesn't get it or, perhaps my guess, doesn't want to.

My friend, who at this point had just returned from Afghanistan said, "Kug, all I ever wanted to be was a Marine. I'm proud of my years of service. But the President said that about not getting paid, all I could think of were those young Privates and PFC's going out on patrol in the morning.

They'll go whether they're paid or not, and they're not paid much. They risk their lives with IED's at every turn. One of them just might come back limbless. For the first time in my career, I asked myself, for what?"

How do you think our military brass feel about sitting in front of the President for a major economic address to the nation when he berates a Senator? Senator Paul Ryan is asked to sit in the first row, front and center. Senator Ryan from Illinois is a new Senator. He had just put forth his own economic recovery plan. I might add Senator Ryan is a Republican. Throughout his entire speech, President Obama berates the man he invited to sit right in front of him.

Obama was incensed that a young Senator and Republican would dare put an economic plan together before he presented his. He wanted to send a message. It said, 'I can crush you'. He loves intimidation as a tactic.

I ask, is that leadership? Is that bringing different views together? What did that say to the Generals in attendance? The Joint Chiefs of Staff, say? It says you do not question me! They had General McCrystal and others as an example. Do you think they'll speak up on the war? Not a chance.

It also shows what a very small person our President is and how very sensitive and petty he is. It speaks to his Chicago Style Politics and his level of immaturity. It devalues the office of the Presidency. It also says he thinks he is above the law. I believe he has no respect for the Office and what we see in his behavior is an indication of his long term plan.

One other item worth commenting on is Wiki Leaks. As I mentioned earlier, Wiki Leaks is an Internet organization founded by a man by the name of Julian Assange. His goals were to find and distribute secrets of governments, namely ours. It hit the airwaves big, by publishing communications between our State Department and other Allies. He also revealed military documentation from Afghanistan.

The leaks barely made a ruffle in the trees mainstream media. Most countries hit by the leaks were miffed, a couple lives of operatives were probably lost, but the story was gone as quickly as it came. No one, including our Commander in Chief seemed to care. Why would that be?

Julian Assange, an Australian citizen and former computer hacker, is wanted in Sweden on a warrant for sexual assault. He is a self appointed whistleblower and activist. He obtained top secret and protected information, from a nation at war and no one but the military says a word.

If you're over forty you'll remember a time when things were much different. Top secret information was secured by a Top Secret clearance. That meant you'd better keep your mouth shut, period. No questions asked. Apparently that is not the case anymore?

Two of my friends, one Air Force and one Marine, served in various forms of intelligence during the Vietnam War. They had the highest forms of clearance. One served in Turkey and one in Vietnam. To this day, they will not discuss what they did, saw, or didn't see. It's not one of those, 'I can't tell you or I'll have to kill you' things either. It's simply the deep respect they have for the oath they took on behalf of America. What happened to that oath? What happened to the enforcement of that oath? Where is our Commander in Chief on the issue?

These documents were leaked by a Private in the United States Army. Why would a Private have access to sensitive material? No one in leadership seems to have asked that question or why he did it. What was his motivation for working with Wiki Leaks and Assange?

Where is the outrage? No mention of the seriousness and illegality of that act of leaking sensitive information to the enemy. But lots of sympathy for the 'poor' Army guy who leaked it. We should try him for treason! Then we should bring Wiki Leaks pervert Julian Assange here and do the same. What has happened to America? Why does our President have no voice on this issue?

In mid-September 2011, General David H. Petraeus retired after a 37-year, decorated career with the US Army. General Petraeus was the man who turned around the war in Iraq. He was then called upon to go to Afghanistan, after President Obama couldn't get along with the first two Generals he personally sent to lead the effort there.

He ended his career by giving an address before a joint review at Fort Meyer in Arlington. Every branch of service was represented, the flags from all fifty states waved in the fall breeze. Many of his classmates from his 1974 class at West Point were in attendance. Many former soldiers he had served throughout his storied career were also there.

Yet there was one, conspicuously, not in attendance. His Commander in Chief and ours, was markedly absent from the General's retirement ceremony. A General who America owes so much ... and his boss couldn't take the time to be there? That says it all.

As we conclude remarks about our Commander in Chief, there is a throng out there saying, "But you give our President no credit or mention for getting Osama Bin Laden!" So rather than give you fuel for your fire, I'm going to comment on it. Here is what my thoughts are:

1. He was the Commander in Chief at the time of the hit by Seal Team 6, so he gets the credit. He presumably made the decision to go for it, and that is surprising, but good.

2. Just as he gets the credit for this one, he gets the credit for the next chapter too. The economic problems he inherited are his ... just like Osama. You can't have it both ways.

3. Remember, the infrastructure that pulled this off was put into place by Bush the Younger. Obama made a good and surprising decision in taking him out.

As they say back in his home country of Africa, the President got his first lion, kind of.

Lastly, as we consider President Obama as Commander in Chief, listen to Donald Trump's remarks regarding his actions and decisions in the Middle East.

"Obama also will continue to pressure Israel unfairly, all the while claiming that he is a true friend of Israel. From the outset of his term, Obama has exerted undue public pressure on Israel to continue making concessions to the Palestinians.

He has also increased aid and military cooperation with the Palestinians despite the Palestinian Authority unifying with the terrorist organization Hamas. Obama even somehow tied his administration's attempts to stop the Iranian nuclear program to progress on the Palestinian question."

The Donald continues, "Further, Obama used the great occasion of killing bin Laden to demand that Israel go back to the indefensible 1976 borders. All this has accomplished are continued demands by the Palestinians and now the rest of the world against Israel, culminating in next week's UN Resolution unilaterally declaring Palestine a sovereign state without any denunciation of terrorism or recognition of Israel's right to exist."

Trump concludes with, "While the Obama administration claims to be fighting the Resolution, he has yet to put any public demands on either the Palestinians or the UN, an institution that America funds with over 22% of its budget. Obama has proven during his term that without America's steadfast and public support, Israel will be placed in a corner by the rest of the world."

Listen to the man. Don't judge him by his TV show, but by what he has achieved. Just one night, wouldn't you love to see a debate between the Donald and the 'Emperor'? That would be the most watched debate ever. What I'd pay to see The Donald hand Barry his head.

Our concern is even higher after the recent debacle with our drone in Iran. We still haven't been told exactly how an intact airplane, one of our most sophisticated drones goes down in one piece in Iran. I would certainly think the brains that can create a drone could make it self destruct if it went into enemy hands?

But they apparently didn't and we believe Iran and Imanutjob have it since they put it on public display. Our President was presented with three options. First was to destroy it in place with an air strike. Second was to send in the SEAL's and retrieve it. And third, do nothing. Our Commander in Chief picked door number three. Isn't that lovely? Of course a week or so later he publically begged for its return.

Our enemy today is the Commander in Chief. He needs to be removed from office before he disarms our entire country. Remember, you cannot challenge the man. Senator Ryan found out, the Generals have found out and read on and you'll see more evidence of our Perfumed Prince and his Dictatorial attitude as we look at his very foreign, foreign policy.

"There must be no doubt that the United States of America welcomes change that advances self-determination and opportunity. Yes, there will be perils that accompany this moment of promise. But after decades of accepting the world as it is in the region, we have a chance to pursue the world as it should be."

President Barack Hussein Obama

While addressing Middle East leaders, praising the Arab uprisings taking place and using the words of his mentor Saul Alinsky, Author of the book 'Rules for Radicals'. The book was dedicated to Satan, the first revolutionary.

Thomas Jefferson and John Adams went to London to wait upon
Tripoli's (Libya today) Ambassador to London in March 1785.
When he arrived they inquired by what right the Barbary states
preyed upon American shipping, enslaving both crews and
passengers? , America's two foremost envoys were informed that "it
was written in the Quran, that all Nations who should not have
acknowledged their authority were sinners, that it was their right
and duty to make war upon whoever they could find and to make
Slaves of all they could take as prisoners, and that every Mussulman
(Pirate) who should be slain in battle was sure to go to Paradise."

History of the Battle of Tripoli
It eventually involved President Jefferson sending
the US Navy and Marines to the north of Africa
to take care of business

A Very Foreign, Foreign Policy

We all knew the guy had no experience. But in our wildest imagination did we expect the Nobel Peace Prize Winner to get us into more wars than he inherited? I don't think so? He was always inconsistent. As a Senator he supported the vote for war in Afghanistan. Apparently it must have been peer pressure because on the Campaign trail he was going to shut it all down immediately if elected.

But none of us could have ever dreamed he would blatantly set out to change American foreign policy as it related to our cherished Allies around the world. He didn't waste any time in setting a new direction for America.

Let's start with the fact he did inherit two wars. Tricky Dick Nixon inherited one big one. Of course Nixon inherited a real mess. He had over 600 known, live POW's, being brutally tortured in North Vietnam. He bombed Hanoi into submission, ending in the Paris Peace Talks. He did all that before displaying his insanity with Watergate.

It wasn't pretty, but then, war is hell. But, he did end the war and brought most of the POW's home. If you don't like wars, then don't send our young men and women to fight unless our National Security is actually at risk. Our outstanding military can be the dogs of war. Don't unleash them if not to fight.

The parallel really ends with the fact that they both inherited wars. Obama inherited a police action in Iraq at that point. In Afghanistan, he inherited a limited and restricted war. The initial assault was done right, prior to Obama arriving. Using surgical strikes and special operations, Bush the Younger went in and destroyed the Taliban and their support of Al Qaeda in retaliation for their strike into the World Trade Center and the Pentagon.

But Commander in Chief Barack didn't bomb anyone into submission. He started out by rewarding some of his supporters with the announcement of the closure of the Liberal hating Guantanamo Bay, and the end to both wars. He followed that with his World Apology Tour. Then, he really took a left turn and returned the bust of Churchill to the British. Thus began the very, very foreign policy of Barack Hussein Obama.

It quickly became clear that the new President had no appreciation for American history, the history of our wars, or in all probability, he didn't know or care.

When we left Vietnam in 1975, millions of South Vietnamese were killed or imprisoned for supporting the United States. The news media conveniently forgets that tragedy. In 2005, thirty years after the war ended, I met a middle aged Vietnamese woman whose father was just then released from a re-education camp in Vietnam. His crime? He was a South Vietnamese Army Officer. The same will happen when we announce our withdrawal from either Iraq or Afghanistan. We have a President who doesn't know the ramifications of his decisions.

Yes, Mr. Obama inherited a mess. And, he jumped right on it. Unlike Mr. Nixon, Obama's moves are more with rhetoric, than action. He didn't load his guns or planes, his Whiz Kids just keep reloading his teleprompter. While he announced the end of torture, he tortured his fellow Americans with a record number of TV appearances.

Mr. Obama's early statements and actions bordered on the absurd. The man who would become President, the man who hadn't run as much as a lemonade stand or led a group of people larger than a Scout Troop, was making decisions that showed his lack of experience, his political paybacks and much worse. Over time the worse began to surface. His actions would begin to show a pattern of the change he really had in mind.

Let's check out his world apology tour. Do you think this might have an impact of foreign policy?

- "My job to the Muslim world is to communicate that the Americans are not your enemy. We sometimes make mistakes. We have not been perfect." Delivered via interview with Al Arabiya, January 27, 2009.

- "In America, there's a failure to appreciate Europe's leading role in the world. Instead of celebrating your dynamic union and seeking to partner with you to meet common challenges, there have been times where America has shown arrogance and been dismissive, even derisive." Delivered in France April 3, 2009.

- "In dealing with terrorism, we can't lose sight of our values and who we are. That's why I closed Guantanamo. That's why I made very clear that we will not engage in certain interrogation practices. I don't believe that there is a contradiction between our security and our values. And when you start sacrificing your values, when you lose yourself, then over the long term that will make you less secure." Delivered in France, April 3, 2009.

- "The United States is still working through some of our own darker periods in our history. Facing the Washington Monument that I spoke of is a memorial of Abraham Lincoln, the man who freed those who were enslaved even after Washington led our Revolution. Our country still struggles with the legacies of slavery and segregation, the past treatment of Native Americans." Delivered in Turkey, April 6, 2009.

- "While the United States has done much to promote peace and prosperity in the hemisphere, we have at times been disengaged, and at times we sought to dictate our terms." Delivered to a meeting of the Americas, April 17, 2009.

- "Don't be discouraged that we have to acknowledge potentially we've made some mistakes." Delivered to CIA employees in Langley, Virginia on April 29, 2009.

- "Unfortunately, faced with an uncertain threat, our government made a series of hasty decisions. I believe that many of these decisions were motivated by a sincere desire to protect the American people. But I also believe that all too often our government made decisions based on fear rather than foresight, that all too often our government trimmed facts and evidence to fit ideological predispositions." Washington, DC, May 21, 2009.

The President was sure busy those first three or four months. He was traveling the world sending messages to his supporters about the New America he was leading. What did he get for it? On October 9, 2009 Barack Obama was awarded the Nobel Peace Prize.

Let's take a look at his early trail of destruction in his, Very Foreign, Foreign Policy:

- Our Man takes office and returns the bust of Churchill given to Bush the Younger at the outset of what was called the War on Terror after 9/11. I'm no Diplomat but where in leadership do you insult our prime, numero uno ally?

The Brit's have always been with us and we with them, until now. As a former truck driver of mine would say, "Ed, I wouldn't slam the shit house door that hard!" There had to be an ulterior motive.

- If that wasn't bad enough, the President then snubs the new British Prime Minister as he visited DC. He didn't make time to meet the man. He said a few words as they cut through the kitchen during a hotel meeting. What a great way for the President of the leading free nation in the world to treat the British.

- Shortly thereafter, in his first few months in office, he makes a similar snub to the Israeli Prime Minister, Benjamin Netanyahu. Why? It wasn't clear, but the snubs continue to this day. The real signal of the Presidents intention came with his demand for Israel to return to pre-1967 borders (more on this later). This one strikes me as particularly malicious since the Israeli's are the only free nation and our only reliable ally in the Middle East. Maybe Mr. Obama has another agenda?

- Look at his non-stop world tour, which continues by the way, apologizing for America's past behavior. It shows this guy really doesn't like America. Perhaps he and his cohorts are setting a new course to correct the past mistakes they see. I guess it's much like our education system, rewriting the history of our country. Is that the change America has been longing for? All I can say, if Obama's World Apology Tour doesn't go right up your butt, then you're not a true American. Period.

- Then his incessant need to suck up to our self-stated enemies, namely Venezuela and Iran. Hugo Chavez in Venezuela is just a bully Dictator. Iran's Ahmadinejad is the world's second leading nut job behind North Korea's Kim Jong-Il. Obama is apparently of the mistaken belief that the world loves him like the American media does.

  Think about this for a moment. Our President is cozying up to these two terrorists at the same time his own Treasury Department, headed by Mr. Turbo Tax himself, Timothy Geithner, is working to freeze billion's in assets of these two countries.

  Who knows, maybe Timothy didn't pass the memo to his boss? What does Geithner know that his boss apparently doesn't? It seems Iran is funneling money for terrorism, not only to Venezuela, but to Hugo's family, and to terrorist groups such as Hamas, Hezbollah, al-Qaida and even the Columbian Revolutionary Armed Forces.

- Of course we couldn't forget his announced wish of committing America to unilateral nuclear disarmament that hides under the name of world nuclear disarmament. You and I both know that the likes of Iran, Venezuela, North Korea, China and Russia cannot be trusted to do what they say.

  Between the beginning of World War II and the early 60's Russia made 53 agreements in the UN or with the US and broke 51 of them. Past behavior is a predictor of future behavior. So why commit our country to such a dangerous position, unless, you have an ulterior motive.

- The fact that our new Commander in Chief calls the war on terror and terrorists by many different names is quite interesting. He's come up with new terms such as violent extremists, overseas contingencies, man-caused disasters and many more. All designed to downplay the significance of the enemy we face. In every case, he avoids the mention of Islam.

  Attorney General Eric Holder, an Obama appointee, without consulting either the FBI or New York City Police, announces he will try the architect of the 9/11 plot in New York Federal Court. That decision to have terrorists tried in Federal Court would have opened our entire government up to the world.

  While he later reversed his decision, the mere intention to do so is very disturbing and shows an incredible weakness, a blatant disregard for our Constitution or an intention to bring down America.

  It was around this time that the President said, "We'll do everything we can to prevent another 9/11." He then went on and explained that if another 9/11 did happen, he was confident we (the American people) could absorb another hit. Isn't that comforting? I'm sure his friends in the sand must love it! Perhaps it was another signal?

- That leads us to the worst terrorist attack on US soil since 9/11 ... the Fort Hood Massacre. Major Nidal Malik of the US Army opens fire on troops who are mustering to head off to the war in Afghanistan. Major Malik murdered 12 and wounded 30. What does our Commander in Chief have to say? "We must resist the temptation to turn this into political theater."

That was his response to the Republicans calling for a Congressional Investigation. A US Army Officer murders 12 people and our President doesn't want an investigation? Could it be that the Officer in question was a Muslim. Think about that for a moment. The same man, our President, wasn't concerned about the 'theater' of having public trials of terrorists in civil courts, but he doesn't want Americans to jump to conclusions on Major Malik?

We'd learn soon after that Major Malik, an Army Psychiatrist, intended to kill as many soldiers as he could ... for Allah! He'd been a long-term performance problem in the Army. Yet because of political correctness, his performance was ignored and he was passed along and even promoted.

He expressed his hatred of Americans; in fact the FBI had been watching him for years. There were even emails government officials were aware of between Major Malik and a radical Imam in Yemen who urges the killing of American troops anywhere.

Now don't blame the Army for not acting on these big red flags. Any Officer who had acted would have seen his career go up in flames for 'discriminating' against the distinguished Major Malik, an Arab and a Muslim. Why?

It's very simple. Political correctness is alive and well and a growth industry in America. I first experienced it in Corporate America. When we set aside special privileges for one group over another, you stifle free speech.

And you lose what I call the 'umbrella of safety' all leaders must provide. It must be okay for me to tell my leader the truth. That is no longer the case anywhere in America.

When you give people the answer they are supposed to say, you will get that answer, and not the truth. That is what Political Correctness does. Our society is now telling us what is okay and not okay as an answer to certain questions. The final report from the Army did not mention or consider the fact Malik was a Muslim, an Arab and had ties to radical Islam. That is the equivalent of Russian roulette.

An aside to the Major Malik story, he is an Arab psychiatrist who is assigned to directly work with Army men and women going to and coming back from war. Maybe we should let the Army know they are fighting Arabs and Muslims. Does that make sense to you?

I have nothing personal against Arabs. I didn't have anything personal against the Vietnamese, who I fought against. But I wouldn't have wanted a Vietnamese psychiatrist talking with me about my problems after the war.

- Does any of this bother you?

Mr. Obama's foreign policy is foreign to the American people. There is something more sinister going on. His actions were questionable, but the picture started taking shape for me as I studied his actions in the so-called Arab Spring.

You've certainly heard about it by now. The news media calls it the March for Freedom in the Arab World, from Tunisia to Bahrain to Egypt, the Sudan and Syria and well, Libya. It's being called a youth revolution led by Google, Twitter and Instant Messaging enthusiasts.

The media and the White House pushed the line that we'll 'all be better for this amazing transformation' taking place in the Middle East. To hear our President tell it, it might as well be the second falling of the Berlin Wall. I wasn't buying it and you shouldn't either. Don't believe a single word. The so called Arab Spring is as orchestrated as the New York Philharmonic.

I've never been a conspiracy theorist and laughed at those who were. It has taken me the past three years to arrive where I am today. The Arab Spring is about as authentic as al-Qaeda being a humanitarian organization.

Let me walk you through what is going on in our world. It's not pretty. We'll take a look at the Arab Spring and our President's response, and how that fits into his very foreign, foreign policy.

- **Tunisia**: I knew Tunisia was in the Middle East but couldn't have told you one thing about it. That is until it blossomed as the first new tulip of the Arab Spring. Supposedly bu a shopkeeper who'd had enough and set himself of fire. The Arab spring was blooming.

  Recent surveys by Al-Jazeera find that 47% of the Tunisians identify with Islam and another 19% Arab Nationalists. The recent election was won by a man proclaiming an Islamic democracy as his goal. Good luck with that one.

- **Egypt**: While a few countries imploded at once, Egypt seemed the most interesting. Since Jimmy Carter and Anwar Sadat sat down with Jordan and made peace a few decades ago, Egypt and Jordan honored its peace with Israel.

  Egypt and Jordan remained allies of the United States, to the extent anyone in that part of the world is an ally to the Great Satan. So I found Obama's reaction to the Egyptian revolution a little, well, 'foreign'.

  I found it 'foreign' because here we were 'urging on the young people' who were fighting to bring down one of our two Middle East allies. Was it really that President Mubarak was a Dictator? I never heard mention of it prior to the revolution.

  If he was a Dictator it certainly wasn't to the extent of say, Iran's nut job, or Hugo in Venezuela or Kim in North Korea. Since the President opposed toppling Saddam, a man who made Mubarak look angelic, why did he then, very publicly, support taking down the leader of Egypt? I just couldn't figure it?

  We didn't know who would replace him. It was easy to see they wouldn't be pro-Israel. Tourism and business in Egypt went down the tubes. In the vacuum of revolution the Muslim Brotherhood stood to gain some significant ground.

  Despite denials by the White House of the 'Brotherhoods' involvement, they were opening the door to them, which is like taking an LA Gang to Scout Camp.

Up to this point, we'd heard it was a revolution of young people. CNN, Fox, MSNBC, you name it. They all reported it as the first social media uprising in history. But shortly after reporting it this way, Fox did begin to change their tune.

The mainstream media made it sound like Twitter and Facebook met Valley Forge! It sounded downright American. The courageous youth were demanding democracy. Now there's an oxymoron.

I couldn't help but wonder where those Arab youth were when our troops rolled into Baghdad, toppling their tyrant for them? Maybe we knocked out Twitter and Google with our Shock and Awe Campaign? The whole idea of an Arab Spring still didn't compute for me.

I didn't get it. Why did our President think this was a good idea? What was different all of a sudden? I had to reboot myself a couple of times, but it started adding up. I may not always be the first horse out of the gate but I run a good race. I do know how to solve problems and my light bulb came on.

Let's make it simple. Ask, who benefits? It's certainly not Israel, the only democracy within a nuclear shot of the Arab world. And the new Sheriff in town made it very clear early on that he wasn't a fan of the Israelis. So he doesn't care what happens to them. So who benefits?

America's biggest problem is we don't know what we get when the revolution is over. Everyone knows the new Egypt will not be honoring Jimmy Carter's peace treaty. So that doesn't work for us. Why doesn't our President see the obvious?

Who benefits? The winner has to be Iran. That's right, the same Iran that is fast developing nuclear weapons and supporting terrorists. They win because our new Sheriff, President Obama, encouraged the 'youth' onward and upward. With a clear signal from Obama, they knew they were home free. They succeeded.

With the Arab Spring rolling in like a breath of fresh camel dung, they're now the unchallenged leader of the Arab world. Iran's garden is blooming. If you doubt this, you doubt it at our own peril. The Arab Spring has sprung and I believe our Mr. Obama just may be the fertilizer they've been looking for.

What makes all this so interesting is that Iran's leader, as Jay Leno calls him, Imanutjob, believes he is the Chief Gardner of this Arab Spring. You see, Islam is anxiously awaiting the arrival of their Big Guy like we await the Second Coming of Jesus Christ. Fair enough. But unlike Jesus Christ, their Big Guy comes not in peace, but amidst violence.

If you're a doubter, it's well documented in the Quran. America needs to wake up and realize there are at least two Quran's. The American version of the Quran is different than the 'Quran' as Muslims know it. Understand that Islam practices deceit to reach their goals, similar to our communist friends.

As the story goes, all the Muslim nations must be under one umbrella and one leader. Smell the flowers of spring. Imanutjob believes he is in for the top job. He believes he'll one day be in charge of all Muslim nations.

Since the Big Guys return is based on violence to us Infidels, well, he believes if he increases violence in the Holy War, he'll hasten the return of their Big Guy, and hence their taking over the world for Islam. It is what they believe.

It's a little like Christians who think if they could learn to love everyone unconditionally, they just might be able to hasten the return of the Savior. Not a bad idea actually.

This is the part of the story where the Politically Correct Police arrive, sirens blazing, screaming, "You're an Islamaphobe!" Am I? Heavens no, I'm a realist. We survived in Vietnam, as I am sure the veterans in all wars did, by knowing our enemies. In the case of Islam, they even tell us they hate us, want to kill us and cut off our heads.

PC Police be damned, if Islam has been hijacked, where are all the prisoners? The ones who are crying out saying I am not part of that! Where are the ones saying I am for America! I've yet to hear one Imam or cleric, at even one Mosque, declare publicly that they do not support the direction of the whole of Islam. They show nothing but allegiance and that speaks volumes about their beliefs.

That is precisely what I believe the Arab Spring is all about. I'm sure there are young people over there genuinely fighting for their freedom. I have no doubt they are a minority and have been duped. I also have no doubt they will never see the freedom they are seeking.

Tunisia and Egypt are two pieces of a big puzzle. Our President's agrees with the direction to drive the 'change' he promised, but never defined. His allegiance and direction becomes a little clearer each day he is in office. If we Americans don't wake up soon, our grandchildren have no chance at the America we loved and enjoyed.

It's all very simple. With the old Egypt gone, the new one is not going to play nice with the Jews. The Middle East is blooming with fires, death and bloodshed. Iran is the winner with a little help from a friend in the White House. Think that couldn't happen here? Reread the chapters on communism.

We have influential people in Hollywood today, people you admire, who still think the Twin Towers were brought down by the CIA! For goodness sakes, Tom Cruise is walking around making weirder statements than I am every day. We must wake up and get involved in saving our country now. We must do it in 2012.

We're already seeing the influence of the Muslim Brotherhood in Egypt. We've seen more deaths and blood running in the once beautiful streets of Cairo than ever before.

Our President has been mum on the issue since the fall of Mubarak. You decide. Read on and we can weep together for the America we love.

- **Libya:** The late Colonel Muammar al-Qaddafi is one strange dude. First off, if you're head of a country, a Dictator no less, why are you just a Colonel? Enquiring minds what to know.

Qaddafi was behind the terrorist bombing of the plane that went down over Lockerbie, Scotland, killing 270 people. He is a bad guy. There is no debating that fact.

He was even worse before President Reagan sent him a wakeup call in the form of two jet fighters that dropped a couple five hundred pounders. They swooped in one morning with a wakeup call of a few five hundred pounder bombs on his house. He remained a bad guy but had a different outlook on the world. He shut his big mouth, left America alone and became a Maverick in his own world.

The Muslim World didn't really like it. He didn't play well with his brothers in the Middle East. Libya's was a country run by a crazy man; but then name one Middle East country that isn't? The leaders of Iran, Syria, Somalia, you name it, they make Hosni Mubarak look good.

The flowers of the Arab Spring began blooming amidst rockets and small arms fire in Libya. To the surprise of most, our anti-war President throws gas on the streets of Tripoli. He openly wants to topple a Dictator, again.

I figured he must be reveling in all the stories told by his friends Bill Ayers and Bernardine Dohrn. He missed their treasonous ways from back in the sixties when they were doing the same thing in our American streets.

Unlike Egypt, where he stood passively by, fanning the flames in the streets of Cairo, Obama wanted a piece of the action in Libya. The Arab League was calling for an intervention to stop the violence. Our new Sheriff was on the case.

The President ignores Congress and goes to the UN for approval. The UN Security Council approves a resolution to act with 'all necessary measures to protect civilians' in Libya. Remember his need to work through the UN for all actions. It is an important part of his 'change plan'.

Obama immediately reinterprets the resolution that it's okay for NATO to become the Libyan Rebel Air Force. The UN's intention was to stop the fighting and protect civilians. The intent was not to support one side or the other.

Needless to say, NATO wasn't happy, China and Russia, who abstained in the Security Council vote, weren't happy. They abstained because the action was intended to simply stop the mad man from killing all his people. But Barack was elated.

Our illustrious President defends his decision by saying he acted on the 'responsibility to protect doctrine' which is part of the United Nations.

It's an important new doctrine for the one world government crowd but it is not part of the doctrine of the United States. We have never used it and it's also rejected by the Brits, Scots and many others.

But our new Sheriff moved ahead with cheers from his one-world-government friends, ignoring Congress and committed air assets to yet a new war front. The new 'responsibility to protect doctrine' has far reaching implications in giving more power to the UN and less to the US. Obama is quietly steering the US in a completely new direction, and the American people at large have no clue.

Another quiet change Obama made also concerns the UN. In March of 2011, the UN Security Council passed Resolution 1970. It referred Colonel Qadafi, when captured, to the International Criminal Court. The ICC as it's called, is very controversial in the US.

The International Criminal Court was created by what is called the Rome Statute. The United States is not and never was a party to the Rome Statute. The ICC, according to the UN, should supersede all country laws. Luckily for us, the Rebels didn't wait to try their leader in any court, they just killed him. But, had they brought him to the ICC, it would have set a very bad precedent for our country.

Emperor Barack obviously considers himself above Congress and our laws. His actions ignored the War Powers Resolution of 1973. Let's make no mistake; the Resolution is very important to our country.

It was passed over the veto of then President Richard Nixon. I'd say it was important to Congress then, but they didn't have a say in it this time. The Resolution specifically prohibits the commitment of our armed forces for more than 60 days without Congressional approval. Period, no questions asked. The only other President to ignore the Resolution was Bill Clinton. In fairness, he was probably distracted with things closer to home.

The President also involved us in Libya against the advice and protests of administration lawyers from both the Pentagon and the Justice Department. He was told by his own lawyers that our actions in Libya were in violation of the 1973 Resolution.

He committed our troops in spite of all the evidence against it. Why would a President do that? Think back to Egypt. Remember, I offered the opinion that what's happening is a piece of the larger puzzle of something bigger coming down in the Middle East. Libya is another piece to the puzzle, and Mr. Obama placed it squarely where it needed to go.

By taking the lead in Libya, we're suddenly leading the parade of Arab Spring. We jump right in with no knowledge of who the 'rebels' really are. Why are we supporting people we don't know, or does our President know them?

I've read in British publications that at least some of the 'freedom fighters' are al-Qaeda. Some are from non-Libyan, Muslim nations.

Yet America is supporting their assault on Libya and their Muslim neighbors are silent. Don't you find that fascinating?

The truth is, the late Colonel Muammar al-Qadafi, was a pain in the sides of the Arab World. He did not play well with others including Iran. To fill the garden for Arab Spring, he needed to go. With the help of Mr. Obama he is gone. A new flag now flies over Tripoli. It is reportedly Al-Qaeda and the Muslim Brotherhood.

It is important to ask yourselves on what basis should we have gotten involved in Libya? Bush the Younger was loudly criticized for the same thing in Iraq. He was criticized by our new Sheriff too. If we're really into liberating people from Dictators then the war in Iraq was right.

How about taking some troops to Africa, Darfur maybe, and helping them. Libya offered no threat to the United States. I ask you to consider the possibility that it is all part of the Presidents changes. It is important!

I can only come to the conclusion that our illustrious new Sheriff is working a plan. The way this came down sends a clear message to Iran, you don't have to worry about us. A radical regime has taken over in Libya, and we helped.

One more country is now in line with Imanutjob's plans for the Big Guy coming back to Iraq. You need to think this through for yourselves. The time is now for America. We cannot continue walking in our sleep and ignoring the facts.

I read Facebook posts with people saying the way we're 'fighting' the Libyan War, using the term loosely, is the right way. Commit no troops and support the freedom fighters. That could very well be right--if they were 'Freedom Fighters'. But they weren't and never will be. They are radical Muslims intent on establishing the entire world as Islam.

We're being duped and political correctness is managing us into oblivion. And by the way, there are reports out of Libya, from our rebel allies, that upwards of 10,000 stinger missiles are missing. Stingers are 'the' weapon to bring down a jetliner. Since some bad guys took over, that missile might be coming soon to a jetliner near you.

Let's turn our attention to another Muslim neighbor, Syria, where the Arab Spring is in full view.

- **Syria:** The road to Damascus has quite a few new potholes. President Bashar al-Assad is hammering his people who are undergoing a 'youth' revolution like many of his neighbors. The Arab Spring has sprung there too, and it's downright bloody. The 'freedom fighters' are taking a hit. In fact lots of hits.

  Where is our President on this issue? He offers a few words here and there but no action. Where is the UN on this issue? Where is the Arab League on this issue? Like our President, they have a few words but no actions.

As for the 'freedom fighters', it's not going very well. They don't have a NATO Air Force at their disposal. They don't have British intelligence at their disposal. The U.N, well, not so much. Why do you think that is?

Their people are being killed by the truckload. The world stands by while Assad prunes his garden, using machine guns on his citizens. The rhetoric fly's in all directions about what a bad guy Assad is.
The King of Jordan, a moderate Arab state, calls for Assad to step down, but he keeps on his brutal pruning. Don't you find that interesting that no one is stepping in?

From a foreign policy perspective, Syria causes more trouble for the U.S. than Libya. Assad is pruning much more aggressively than Qadafi did. But I have a hunch here, just a hunch.

I think Iran's Imanutjob likes President Assad. He must, he provides him weapons. It's a good bet that Assad is waiting for the same Big Guy that Imanutjob is ... so, you know where I'm going with this, the Muslims don't want him out. He fits with the coalition they are working towards.

- Does any of this bother you?

- **Pakistan:** It's an interesting nation that gives us an interesting problem. We give $2 billion dollars as year in aid to Pakistan and have no word in how they spend it. In return they 'allow' us to provide support to the Afghan War from their country. Are they allies? Just a little worse than Saudi Arabia. Let's take a look:

- In June 2008 Afghan officials foiled a plot involving ISI to assassinate Afghani President Harnid Karzai.

- The Pakistani ISI, like our CIA, is their major intelligence organization. In July 2008 they were tied to an attack on the Indian Embassy in Kabal, Afghanistan that killed 58 and wounded 141.

- In November 2008 a Pakistani based terrorist organization attacked Mumbai, India killing 164 and wounding another 308.

- In December 2009 a Pakistani suicide bomber killed seven CIA operatives in Khost, Afghanistan.

All of these attacks and many more are tied to what is known as the Haqqani Terrorist Network. The network originated in Afghanistan during their war with Russia. It was set up and funded by both the CIA and the ISI. The purpose of the collaboration was to force the Russians to leave Afghanistan. Today the ISI continues to support the network against the US. It is believed to be based in the Pakistani mountains and receives support from the ISI.

You must vote in 2012 and you must vote to get Obama out of office. If we don't, say goodbye to America. Let's take a look at the one rose in a garden of thorn's ... Israel. But our President doesn't see it that way.

- **Israel:** Following World War II and the United Nations decision to create a Jewish state, David Ben-Gurion declared Israel an independent country. That took place on May 14, 1948.

The next day the Muslim states surrounding Israel attacked. It has yet to stop.

They sit amongst Muslim nations on all sides who vow to kill them. The Muslims proclaim on a regular basis they want to destroy them from the face of the earth. They blame every problem in the world, large or small, on the Jews.

The country of Israel, at points no wider than a trip to your nearest Wal-Mart, is surrounded by stated enemies on all sides. When the Jewish people took over, they had a desert. From that desert, they created an oasis of freedom. It is the only free country in the Middle East.

They have also been our only real ally in that part of the world since their inception. They are a smart and energetic people with a professional military and the world's best intelligence agency.

So why does our new President hate them? He treats them like our own worst enemy. They have stood with us both publicly and privately through all struggles and triumphs. We are the only reason they still exist as a country. Yet, our new man in the White House is dumping them like we have no history.

President Obama regularly snubs Israeli Prime Minister Benjamin Netanyahu. He's done it more than once. He recently was caught in a derogatory exchange off camera with French President Nicolas Sarkozy. They were both running down Israel when they thought the camera was off.

When our President made the call to Israel to go back to its pre-1967 borders, I was furious. I couldn't sleep, it upset me so bad. My PTSD shifted into red rage, as we used to call it.

A sitting American President who publicly proclaims that position, with the intention of backing it at the UN, was too much for me. His remarks preceded the Palestinians' effort to gain recognition at the United Nations. He wasn't fooling me; it was a clear message to them of his support. He hadn't read the tea leaves in America too well, and the backlash was volcanic. He suddenly backed off his position.

He then came out and said he was 'misinterpreted'. His comments left no room for misinterpretation. Our President is doing all he can to lay the ground work for the destruction of Israel and the advancement of Islam.

A few days later, Prime Minister Benjamin Netanyahu was in the States to address Congress. I listened to him in an interview with Piers Morgan. What a delightful, confident and intelligent man. He stated his case and took it to Congress. He is a class act. He openly moves people to action.

Obama on the other hand, showed his cunning, crass and deceitful self. Why would he do that? He has a plan for change alright, but not the one the 51% of Americans who voted for him think.
Watch carefully over the months leading to the election, and see what our Main Man says about Israel, the Arab Spring and the wars in Iraq and Afghanistan. He will sing a different tune.

In spite of all the evidence above, President Obama shows not a hint of shame in saying he is Israel's best friend. Speaking to prominent Jewish supporters at a New York City fundraiser on December 1, 2011 he said, "I try not to pat myself too much on the back, but this administration has done more for the security of the state of Israel than any previous administration."

How you vote this year will make a difference in the future of our grandchildren's lives. You must act! Obama's plans for a brave new world don't include the one we know and love. It leads to Socialism and a one world government.

- **Iraq:** We've been providing security now for a couple years. The war has been over. But the country isn't stable. The government cannot hold their own with Iran next door.

The Wall Street Journal reported on November 7, 2011 that Iraq's Security Forces are already breaking apart along religious lines. Prime Minister Nouri al-Maliki has been purging the Security Forces of anyone with any ties to the Sunni led regime of Saddam Hussein. The Prime Minister is a Shiite. It has only just begun.

Yet Obama announced recently he is bringing all troops home by the end of 2011. Do you think he cares about what happens when we pull out? I think he cares about paying political debts and winning reelection.
Watch for Vietnam like retribution when we pull out of Iraq. Our supporters will die. Then it will become another satellite of Iran.

- **Saudi Arabia:** Admittedly, the Saudi's are the only Muslim country to even act as if they have a genuine interest in America. They did support Bush the Older when we returned Kuwait to its people. Yet, we must remember that all but 4 of the 19 killers on 9/11 were from Saudi Arabia.

  It's also important to understand how they react when challenged, similar to our President. A Canadian organization by the name of EthicalOil.org is committed to promoting the Canadian oil sands as an alternative to getting oil from the OPEC Dictatorships.

  Ethical.org produced a 30 second TV commercial comparing the treatment of women in Saudi Arabia, where women can't drive, vote, or get medical care without their husband's approval, to that of Canada. The Saudi's took serious exception to that. They hired one of the world's largest law firms, Norton Rose, with 2600 lawyers, to silence the Canadian media. Did it work?

  The law firm has been calling news stations across Canada threatening them with law suits if they didn't stop airing the EthicalOil.org ads. Two stations have pulled the ads, one being Canada's largest private broadcaster CTV.

  Saudi Billionaire Prince Walid bin Talal said it is not in the Saudi's best interest to let the price of oil get too high because it could lead to alternative sources of oil. That is why they have a problem with the Canadians; they are creative and have oil.

Conclusion:

America has always been the beacon of light for a free world. America, the one Obama hates, has left bodies of her young on foreign shores its entire history. We have always led the fight for freedom.

Europe would be speaking German without the brave men and women of these United States of America. The rest of the world could very well be speaking Japanese without us. Without the US consumption of oil the Arab states would be left with nothing but sand. They have done nothing with their wealth. They have only helped the ruling families and not their people. We need not be ashamed of these facts, nor should we rewrite them to please a generation of Americans who fail to remember their roots.

The foreign policy of Barack Hussein Obama is a foreign policy to end America as we know it. There is no doubt in my mind that is true. When you compare his words and his actions, they do not match.

While that is common for most politicians, this guy is different. When you look at his decisions, his friends and his staff, you have to be concerned. When you look at his actions since taking office, it is a cause for alarm. What it means for America as we know it isn't good.

We elected a guy we knew nothing about. We elected a guy with no leadership background and no accomplishments. We elected him in a time when our country values appearance over substance. We elected him not knowing he is someone's Trojan horse. We elected him, and he is methodically taking our nation to a place we do not know or want.

Obama will use any method to get what he wants, even if it means allowing the infiltration of our borders.

We must vote him out in 2012!

"Of course, not all my conversations in immigrant communities follow this easy pattern. In the wake of 9/11, my meetings with Arab and Pakistani Americans, for example, have a more urgent quality, for the stories of detentions and FBI questioning and hard stares from neighbors have shaken their sense of security and belonging. They have been reminded that the history of immigration in this country has a dark underbelly; they need specific reassurances that their citizenship really means something, that America has learned the right lessons from the Japanese internments during World War II, and that I will stand with them should the political winds shift in an ugly direction."

President Barack Hussein Obama
From page 261 – Audacity of Hope by Barack Obama

"*The first consideration in immigration is the welfare of the receiving nation. In a new government based on principles unfamiliar to the rest of the world and resting on the sentiments of the people themselves, the influx of a large number of new immigrants unaccustomed to the government of a free society could be detrimental to that society. Immigration, therefore, must be approached carefully and cautiously.*"

Thomas Jefferson

America – The Muslim Nation?

"You might say that America is a Muslim nation." Our main man made that statement back in 2009 while speaking to an audience in Egypt. Say what? What America are you talking about? Before 9/11 the most I'd heard of Muslim's in America was when a lady down the street from us was beheaded for leaving her husband. She turned out to be Muslim. They left her head on the lawn. It sort of freaked out the neighborhood.

We lived in Allen Park, Michigan at the time. It borders Dearborn which I now understand is the largest Muslim community in America. It was around 1979, and it didn't shock me as much as learning we are a Muslim country did. That was shocking and puzzling coming from our President.

Mr. Obama followed that up on the same tour, while speaking in Turkey, by saying, "We Americans do not consider ourselves a Christian nation, or a Muslim nation, but rather, a nation of citizens who are, uh, bound by a set of values."

If he is saying these kinds of things in public, what is he saying in private meetings with his brother Muslims? I couldn't believe my eyes or my ears, but it was all true. It made me think once again, who is this guy?

He had made some outrageous statements on his World Apology Tour, so it wasn't like we should have been so surprised. He had some good ones, that's for sure:

- "America has been arrogant."

Gee, we're the leading country in the world when it comes to giving and supporting countries hit by natural disasters.

Check and see exactly how many Muslim countries are at the top of the giving list. How about Russia and China? I'm sorry but maybe a little arrogance is warranted.

- "After 9/11, America didn't always live up to her ideals."

I wonder exactly which ideals he thinks we didn't live up to. Perhaps protecting our citizens from terrorism by kicking the Taliban's rear end? Maybe it's helping the people in Haiti and Japan when natural disasters strike?

It's become routine for the President to talk softly to the Muslim world and talk tough to ours. Of course, he's the same man who apologies to everyone outside our borders for our behavior and has a wife who is only now proud of her country since her husband took office. And this would be 'the country' that allowed both of them to attend universities they were not qualified to attend. What a bad country we are.

Let's take a quick look at the President's early life as we know it. You know he doesn't share a lot.

- At the age of 6 Obama, then Barry Soetoro, moved to Indonesia with his Mother and Step-Father.

- He attended Catholic school for grades 1-3.

- His family moved within Indonesia, and Barry spent grades 3 and 4 at a Madrasah known as the Besuki School.

- He returned to Hawaii where he went to public school.

- After graduating high school, he attended Occidental College for two years. It was while he attended Occidental in 1980 that he decided to not be Barry Soetoro and went back to Barack Hussein Obama.

- While attending Occidental College in the summer of 1981, Obama traveled to Jakarta, Indonesia, to visit his mother and sister Maya. He also visited friends in Hyderabad, India, and Karachi, Pakistan, for three weeks. I wonder what nations passport he used?

- He transferred from Occidental College to Columbia University where he graduated.

- Following college graduation, he worked in Chicago for the Developing Communities Project. It is a non-profit organization at the time supporting primarily 8 Catholic dioceses.

- In the summer of 1988, Barry, now Barack traveled to Europe for the first time and spent three weeks. He then traveled to Africa to visit relatives for five weeks.

- Obama returned from his travels and attended Harvard Law School. While attending Harvard, he spent 8 days in Los Angeles attending a national course on the Alinsky methods of organizing. (More Alinsky later in this chapter.)

- Following Harvard Law School, Obama returned to Chicago. The actual time he began attending the Reverend Jeremiah Wrights Trinity United Church of Christ is unclear.

However by his own admission in 2008, he had attended his church for over twenty years.

- Since becoming President, it is unclear that he attends any church regularly since denouncing his relationship with Reverend Wright during the campaign.

- President Obama publicly attended church in September of 2010 for the first time in nearly six months, and shortly after a major survey showed that only a third of Americans can correctly identify Obama's faith as Christian. They attended service at St. John's Church Lafayette Square, an Episcopal congregation about a block from the White House.

- On Easter 2011 Obama attended the Shiloh Baptist Church.

Is it any surprise that few people in America can identify the religion of our President? He doesn't regularly attend church anywhere. His last real commitment to church was with the Reverend Wright. Here are a few things Obama must have heard in the twenty years he sat in Mr. Wright's congregation in Chicago.

- "The government gives them the drugs, builds bigger prisons, passes a three-strike law and then wants us to sing 'God Bless America.' No, no, no, God damn America, that's in the Bible for killing innocent people, God damn America for treating our citizens as less than human. God damn America for as long as she acts like she is God and she is supreme."Americans should not sing 'God Bless America' but rather 'God Damn America'."

- "We bombed Hiroshima. We bombed Nagasaki and we nuked far more than the thousands in New York and the Pentagon and we never batted an eye.

  We have supported state terrorism against the Palestinians and black South Africans and now we are indignant because the stuff we have done overseas is now brought back into our own front yards. America's chickens are coming home to roost."

- "America is still the No. 1 killer in the world. ... We are deeply involved in the importing of drugs, the exporting of guns and the training of professional killers. ... We believe in white supremacy and black inferiority and believe it more than we believe in God. ... We supported Zionism shamelessly while ignoring the Palestinians and branding anybody who spoke out against it as being anti-Semitic. ... We started the AIDS virus. ... We are only able to maintain our level of living by making sure that Third World people live in grinding poverty."

Umm? The President says we are a Muslim nation, his Pastor hates America, Obama goes on a World Apology Tour and Israel is now our enemy? What do you think? There appears to be something bigger going on here than we hear about in the press. Let's look a little further and see what all this might mean.

Before we go much further, I want to double back on Obama's training in the Alinsky method of organizing. The Alinsky method originated with a man by the name of Saul Alinsky. Mr. Alinsky is a graduate of the University of Chicago and is sometimes called the Father of Community Organizing in America.

As I mentioned earlier, Mr. Alinsky taught, "True revolutionaries do not flaunt their radicalism. They cut their hair, put on suits and infiltrate the system from within." According to his son, Alinsky viewed revolution as a slow, patient process. The trick was to penetrate existing institutions such as churches, unions and political parties.

Does that at all sound like Marx? Well, there's more. One journalist wrote, "Obama is also an Alinskyite. Obama spent years teaching workshops on the Alinsky method. In 1985 he began a four-year stint as a community organizer in Chicago, working for an Alinskyite group called the Developing Communities Project. Camouflage is the key to Alinsky-style organizing. While trying to build coalitions of black churches in Chicago, Obama caught flak for not attending church himself. He became an instant churchgoer." Isn't that fascinating?

In a letter from David Alinsky, son of the famous Saul, he wrote on what would have been his father's 100th birthday, "Obama learned his lesson well. I am proud to see that my father's model for organizing is being applied successfully beyond local community organizing to affect the Democratic campaign in 2008. It is a fine tribute to Saul Alinsky as we approach his 100th birthday." Now that's special.

We are asleep folks! Obama helped support this organization through the Woods Fund, a non-profit on which Obama served as paid director from 1999 to December 2002. Obama sat on the Woods Fund board alongside William Ayers, founder of the Weather Underground domestic terrorist organization. They provided startup funding and later capital to the Midwest Academy.

The Midwest Academy describes itself as 'one of the nation's oldest and best-known schools for community organizations, citizen organizations and individuals committed to progressive social change.'

Keep in mind the use of 'progressive' today was a 'socialist' in years past. The Midwest Academy teaches the Alinsky tactics of community organizing. Does any of this provide a piece to your puzzle as to what kind of a President we have and who he really is? Well, there's a lot more to come.

Why do you think Obama said we were a Muslim nation, a non-Christian nation? The math doesn't work out, that's for sure. Let's look at Mormons for instance. There are around 7 million Mormons living in the United States. There are maybe 3 million Muslims legally in the United States. That means Mormons outnumber Muslims at least two to one. Maybe this is a Mormon nation? There are over 78 million Catholics in the US. That's a lot more than 3 million? Maybe we're a Catholic nation? No, the President says not.

Do the math folks. Muslims are about 0.003%, that is three tenths of one percent of the population, and our President calls us a 'Muslim Nation'. For goodness sakes, it's as much a Hare Krishna Nation as it is a Muslim. His statement isn't based on fact. In the latest surveys, 70% of Americans identify themselves as Christians. Why would he say such a thing? Why, because he likes to send messages to his brothers around the Muslim world.

He is leading a country that identifies itself as 70% Christian and he has no interest in Christian issues. He has a lot of interest in Muslim issues around the world though. Let's take a look at opportunities to speak out for Christians.

- Take the case of a lady by the name of Asia Bibi Noreen. She sat in a prison cell in Pakistan, you know our ally in the war on terror, for over 15 months. It seems they have some harsh laws against Christians over there. She was accused of badmouthing Muhammad and Islam.

The court didn't want to hear her story, she's a woman you know, and she was convicted and sentenced to death.

She's trying for a Presidential pardon but fat chance. An appeals court blocked the pardon. Even if she were successful, she doesn't face a bowl of cherries. One Muslim cleric has offered a $6,000 reward to anyone who kills her. Could it happen? In a ten year span, our brothers in Pakistan killed 34 people under their 'blasphemy laws', of which 16 were Christians.

- In Bethlehem, the home of the Christian religion, Christians are declining faster than Obama's approval rating. Estimates run from a once high of 80% to today's 20% for Christians living there.

- In the Palestinian territories, Christians are estimated to be less than 2%.

- Open Door USA, a ministry fighting the persecution of Christians around the world, names North Korea, Iran, Saudi Arabia, Somalia, Mauritania, Laos and Uzbekistan as the most dangerous place to be a Christian. How many of those countries are Muslim or Communist? I thought so.

- Pakistan has been pushing a UN resolution since 1999, specifically calling for it to be a crime to defame or discriminate against Islam. The original title of the resolution was the Defamation of Islam resolution.

- Hamas, that great organization of terrorists our President holds sympathy for, issued an edict in Gaza that all female students must wear an Islamic uniform that covers their heads and legs completely.
  Keep in mind that Hamas is a terrorist organization, and now a political party in Gaza.

- Also, in Gaza, militants have vandalized a monastery, Christian and Western School and bombed other western organizations.

- In the West Bank, one man fled after death threats for not giving his land to a Muslim who requested it. Another fled to Canada with his family after being forced to sell his business to Muslim buyers at a fraction of its worth.

In many parts of the world it is tough being a Christian. Did you ever here our President utter even one word in support of Christians anywhere? Me neither. Do you see a problem here? Let's look at a few comments he's made about Muslim's and Christians. I've used bold and italics to show his statements on Christians.

- "We will encourage more Americans to study in Muslim communities".

- *"Whatever we once were, we are no longer a Christian nation."*

- "Islam has always been a part of America."

- *"We do not consider ourselves a Christian nation".*

- "I look forward to hosting an Iftar dinner celebrating Ramadan here at the White House later this week, and wish you a blessed month".

- *Which passages of scripture should guide our public policy? Should we go with Leviticus, which suggests slavery is OK and that eating shellfish is an abomination? Or we could go with Deuteronomy, which suggests stoning your child if he strays from the faith?"*

I once had a picture on our wall which read, "If you were accused of being a Christian, would there be enough evidence to prove it?" Good question for all of us and an excellent question for our President.

Barack Obama would have a very hard time in court proving he is a Christian. The simple reason is that he is not. He is the enemy. He is also our President. If we do not wake up we will pay a price higher than this nation has ever paid. Why does he say this is a Muslim country when at one time he claimed to be a Christian?

- Our President did attend a Muslim school when he was in grade school. That doesn't make him bad, but it is a fact. He recalled the opening lines of the Muslim call to prayer, reciting them with a first-rate accent. In a remark that seemed delightfully off the cuff, Mr. Obama described the call to prayer as "one of the prettiest sounds on Earth at sunset."

- Our President did attend the Reverend Wright's church, for twenty years. The Reverend Wright preaches anti-American hate and revolution.

But when he ran for President, he suddenly did not like that church anymore and doesn't remember any of its teachings.

- The President has said, "You might say that America is a Muslim Nation." *When in fact there is no evidence to that effect.*

- The President has said, "We are no longer just a Christian Nation." *When in fact there is overwhelming evidence to the contrary.*

- The President cancelled our National Day of Prayer in his first year in office. *Yet he openly celebrates every Muslim holiday.*

- The President attended and was photographed attending a Ramadan prayer service for Muslims, kneeling with his shoes off. *Near the time he cancelled the National Day of Prayer.*

- The President bowed, whether he calls it that or not, to the King of Saudi Arabia. *The President is the first US President to do so.*

- Our President continues to reach out to Muslims and Muslim nations but pays no attention to Christian issues around the world *The President is Johnnie on the Spot when it comes to Muslim issues. When is the last time you heard him speak out against Christian persecution?*

- The President, the example of leadership to the free world and all of our children, does not attend church, although proclaiming his Christianity.

Finally, on Easter of 2011 he attends a church service at a church described as preaching doctrine very similar to Jeremiah Wright. *Please note that his church attendance has picked up since he is now in re-election mode.*

- The President's actions regarding world issues speak volumes about his beliefs, more so than his words. *If you listen carefully to his words and who he supports it quickly becomes clear he supports the far left, Islam and socialism. Listen for the fine print in his commentary.*

What does the evidence show? It shows he is more Muslim than Christian, that's for sure. Bring a Muslim and President of the United States is not the issue. The issue is he was elected as a Christian. It's time he comes out of his closet and is judged for his actions, not his words.

What is the state of America right now as it relates to Islam? First, let's look at Islam. Muslim countries are not free. Yet Muslims come here demanding our freedoms with their laws. In Texas, many people have already heard of the Muslims who bought land next to an existing pig farm. Once they moved in, they're petitioning to have the pig farmer removed so they can build a Mosque. The farmer is now holding pig races each Friday. Good for him.

We have Oklahoma judges shooting down citizens in favor of Sharia Law and Minnesota cab drivers demanding they not pick up drunks and the courts side with the Muslims? They are demanding they have a right to behave here as they do in their home countries. If they are Americans, then they need to stand up and be Americans.

It's all part of the plan. It's another piece in the puzzle, and they're fitting perfectly into place. We must decide as Americans where it stops. It must stop with each and every one of us not tolerating the infiltration of our country any longer. Now is the time to stand up and stop it.

Oh boy, the PC Police are on the way, sirens blaring. They're rewriting history and gaining new ground every day. It's socialism or bust and President, Barack Obama is the closer in this age old game.

Political correctness is the enabling tool that pumps life into these changes in the name of tolerance. The tolerance they preach provides protection for the eventual socialization of America. Do not misjudge this one. It is real.

I was speaking to a Middle School in Missoula, Montana, a while back with a Navy fighter pilot from the war in Vietnam. We were killing time between classes. While walking around the foyer, we noticed pictures the students had drawn hanging on the walls.

Shocked wouldn't describe our reaction when we realized the entire interior of a massive foyer was papered in the student's interpretations of the Books of the Quran. We were outraged! We found out later it was a course of study at the school. They were studying a religion that makes up less than three tenths of one percent of our country's population. And that is in Montana!

Can you imagine a class in Middle School studying the Books of the Bible? The ACLU would be there before you could say Matthew, Luke and John. Imagine what they're studying in California. That is absurd. And that is the problem we are facing. The infiltration already runs deep and wide.

America, we're a ticking time bomb in more ways than one. I'm just a citizen crying out because I love this country and what it stands for. We must realize that the enemy is within and we're holding the door wide open. We must close and bolt that door!

Before you go all Postal on me, let me say this first. If the man ran as a Muslim and won the White House, God bless him, or in his case Allah. That is what I and millions of Americans fought for, the American Dream where we can all achieve what we set out to do.

But that is not the case with Mr. Obama. His actions are screaming something very different than his words proclaim. You can't have it both ways. The direction he is taking our country is, in the least, very sympathetic towards Islam, and in the worst, he is performing an inside job for someone. I believe the evidence shows the latter.

President Obama supports the Muslim Brotherhood. He wants to establish relations with them. The Muslim Brotherhood was founded in Egypt in 1928. They collaborated with Nazi Germany and had their hands in terrorism as far back as the 40's and 50's. They were suppressed for the most part until the latest Arab Spring.

Thanks to our Presidents support of the Egyptian uprising against Mubarak, the Muslim Brotherhood is again in power in Egypt. The Brotherhood is always trying to enhance its image in North America and our media and laws help their cause, as does the man now holding the White House.

We need to act now! I am not a nut case. I was not a birther. I was not a conspiracy theorist. I have never been an Islamaphobe. I believe Muslims are welcome in this country like anyone else. Provided they want to be part of it and not make us part of them. They have yet to prove their intentions.

I was originally only upset that a man was elected to the White House with zero credentials and a sketchy background. Now I am upset that we have a man in the White House who is committed to bringing down our democracy.

Candidate Obama and President Obama are distinctly two different people. He is also the best friend the Muslims have ever had in the White House. He is also a Socialist. We can't ignore it. Our country is at stake.

And this man welcomes in our new, old enemy.

*"When we think of the major threats to our
national security, the first to come to mind
are nuclear proliferation, rogue states and global terrorism.
But another kind of threat lurks beyond our shores, one from nature,
not humans - an avian flu pandemic."*

President Barack Hussein Obama

"To take from one because it is thought that his own industry and that of his father's has acquired too much, in order to spare to others, who, or whose fathers, have not exercised equal industry and skill, is to violate arbitrarily the first principle of association — the guarantee to every one of a free exercise of his industry and the fruits acquired by it."

Thomas Jefferson

A New Enemy Arrives, Don't Tell Anyone

I wonder if you have heard about an Advisor to the Department of Homeland Security by the name of Mohammed Elibiary. He is a Muslim and no stranger to controversy. While speaking at a 2004 Texas conference honoring Iran's notorious Ayatollah Khomeini, Mr. Elibiary described him as a 'great Islamic visionary'.

Elibiary has also written in praise of one of the most influential Islamic radicals of the modern era: former Muslim Brotherhood leader, Sayyid Qutb. He speaks out in support of Hamas fundraisers too. He physically threatened a *Dallas Morning News* editor during an email exchange they were having.

In spite of his interesting past, Elibiary sells himself as a moderate expert on Muslim de-radicalization. Why is this important? Our illustrious head of Homeland Security took notice. Napalitano recruited him to be one of 26 Advisors setting direction for the Obama administrations counter-terrorism strategy. Does that concern you?

The only report I could find on Elibiary came from CBN News, the Christian Broadcast Network. Elibiary, as an Advisor to the Department of Homeland Security, and was given access to sensitive documents. Out of 26 members on the Department of Homeland Security's Advisory Council, only Elibiary was granted access to a nationwide database that includes terror watch lists and sensitive FBI reports.

It's unclear why Elibiary was given this special privilege -- but he now finds himself in hot water. The Texas Muslim activist is accused of leaking some of those documents to the media to spread charges of "Islamophobia." At least one lawmaker on Capitol Hill is demanding answers. Yet only CBN is reporting on the story. Why is that?

According to CBN he's accused of taking confidential documents from the Texas Department of Public Safety and shopping them to the media. His reported goal was to damage Texas governor and GOP presidential candidate Rick Perry by showing the so-called, "Islamophobia" of Texas government agencies.

"Within hours of getting access he had downloaded those documents and began marketing to these publications," investigative journalist Patrick Poole, told CBN News. Elibiary was trying to sell the information to the press. Poole broke the story at PJMedia.com after being tipped off by one of the publications about Elibiary's alleged plans. "Oddly enough, Elibiary sits on the Texas Department of Public Safety Advisory Council," Poole said. "This was his own agency that he was sabotaging -- or trying to sabotage."

We should start by asking why Director of Homeland Security, Janet Napolitano, would appoint such a person to a key intelligence and strategic post. Especially, since he is on the record, speaking praise on behalf of our enemies. We could follow that up by asking why he was allowed access to sensitive information. Of 26 Advisors to Napolitano, why does he get special treatment? We probably wouldn't get any answers either.

Texas Republican Representative Louie Gohmer said, "And Napolitano puts the guy on the Homeland Security Advisory Committee, gives him a secret clearance?" Gohmer wants an investigation into the Elibiary leak case. He grilled Napolitano about it on Capitol Hill last month during a congressional hearing. At the time, she promised to 'look into it'.

Gohmert later told CBN News the Elibiary incident reflects a larger problem of radical Islamists, including some linked to the Muslim Brotherhood, advising the U.S. government on its counterterrorism policies.

"They're bringing in the Muslim Brotherhood to the inner sanctum and saying 'Look, they like us! This means peace in our time!' And what they're doing is subjecting this nation to real danger," he said. Elibiary's access to the Homeland Security database has reportedly been revoked since the scandal broke.

- Does that bother you?

It should go right up your butt like a bottle rocket. It should scare you straight, straight to the voting booth in 2012. You keep thinking about the story above while we take a look at what this peaceful Muslim religion teaches about deception.

The deceptions like Mr. Elibiary used are common to what Islam is using on us in the West. The countries of Europe are already living the fruits of that deception, as they watch Islam devour their cultures like a ravenous vulture. The vultures are circling America right now. A few like Fort Hood's Major Nidal Malik and Mr. Mohammad Elibiary have landed and begun their work.

Reading from Muslim holy works in Sunna Abu Dawud, Book 14, Number 2631, narrated by Ka'b ibn Malik we find the words of the Prophet Mohammad declaring, "War is deception." Jihad is war to Muslims. Jihad is both a personal war to serve Allah and a war against non-believers. War to Mohammad was deception.

It is difficult for us in the West to accept such a concept. We have our Christian belief which teaches us to trust others, and turn the other cheek. Now we have a government pushing political correctness on us and telling us what to think. It is part of the plan.

There is a command in Islam known as Kitman (lying by omission). It is a command to deliberately conceal the truth to mislead an enemy of Islam.

It is primarily practiced by Shi'a Muslims, but it is a legal, righteous practice for any Muslim. Imam Jafar Sadiz, the sixth Imam of Shi'a Islam says: "One who exposes something from our religion is like one who intentionally kills us. You belong to a religion that whosoever conceals it, Allah will honor him and whosoever reveals it, Allah will disgrace him."

These are facts. We should judge Mr. Malik and Mr. Elibiary by their acts. They are in line with Muslim teachings. My opinion is not about Islamophobia - it's about due diligence to protect our country. I wish I could say the same about our Head of Homeland Security or our Defense Secretary Robert Gates. When Major Malik killed the troops in Fort Hood he later referred to it as 'workplace' violence. We cannot be deceived any longer. The time is growing short for us to act.

Many will argue I'm cherry picking a few teachings of Islam and calling them their beliefs. Deception is part of the plan of Islam. Let's look at their actions as well as their teachings. Consider these acts against the people of America.

- The first to come to mind of course are the hijackers of 9-11. They lived amongst us, pretended to be our friends and killed over 3,000 of our citizens.

- The Saudis pretend to be our ally. They even help us at times. Yet, the majority of the killers of 9-11 were Saudi citizens.

- After the attacks on 9-11 there was a survey taken of British Muslims. They found only 17% believed any Muslims were involved in 9/11 and 57% believe there were no Muslims involved. Yet they marched in the London streets with banners reading, 'the Magnificent Nineteen'.

- Major Malik pretended to be a US Army Officer, a psychiatrist, and murdered more than a dozen servicemen and women at Fort Hood.

- Elibiary, who we talked about at the beginning of this chapter, worked his way into the Department of Homeland Security by pretending to be a consultant in Muslim de-radicalization.

- US Army Private Naser Abdo, a Fort Campbell soldier, was recently arrested in Killeen, Texas for plotting to kill soldiers there. Private Abdo joined the Army in 2009 and in 2010 after receiving orders for Afghanistan declared conscientious objector status. Before that was granted he was found in possession of child pornography and kicked out of the service. An alert gun owner in Killeen tipped off police and they discovered the plot.

- There are many other examples of terrorists plots foiled where Muslims were hiding amongst us.

We'll look at another word used in Muslim theology is 'al-Taqiyya' (an outright lie). That is according to A Shiite Encyclopedia, October 1995, and revised January 2001. The word 'al-Taqiyya' literally means, "Concealing or disguising one's beliefs, convictions, ideas, feelings, opinions, and/or strategies at a time of imminent danger, whether now or later in time, to save oneself from physical/or mental injury."

Understand that we're dealing with an enemy with one value – allegiance to Allah, an enemy with one goal - global Jihad and world dominance. That sounds familiar. We read about the communists who have a similar goal. Isn't that interesting?

We must understand that whether its communism, Islam or perhaps a combination of the two, they can and will do anything that gets them closer to their goals. For Muslims or Communists, these beliefs are especially important for them when working in countries where they are the minority.

In the Quran, which is a part of Muslim scripture, it says, "Anyone who, after accepting faith in Allah, utters unbelief, except under 'compulsion', his heart remaining firm in faith – but such as open their breast to unbelief, on them is wrath from Allah, and theirs will be a dreadful penalty". (Sura 16:106)

Sura means 'book', like 'Mark' or 'John' in the Bible. The Suras are individually named and are all in the Quran. The Sunna and Hadith are observations and quotes of the Prophet Muhammad's speech and habits that are from his followers and not in the Quran. The Quran, Hadith, and Sunna are the three spiritual, legal, moral, and social guides in Islam.

The operative word in the Sura above is 'compulsion'. Meaning you can deny the faith here in America where you are a minority, as long as it is to deceive. But, if you happen to leave the faith entirely, shame on you, it's actually death on you. We're dealing with an enemy within who arrived by deceit. Our new enemy swooped in under the veil of political correctness with a little help from his friends. In our culture it is very difficult to address these issues. We must find a way.

I am sure there are Muslims who want peace. The problem is discovering the difference between those who want us dead and those who don't. When we look purely at behavior as it relates to actions against the United States we don't have to look far. There are a string of acts of war and crimes by Muslims that we must consider. While this is a long list – we need to read it and let it sink in.

- 1979 - Iran Hostage Crisis: seizure of US Tehran Embassy, Iran November 4, 1979 for 444 days.

- 1983 - Bombing of US Beirut Embassy, Lebanon - April 18, 1983.

- 1983 - Bombing of US Marine barracks, Beirut, Lebanon - October 23, 1983.

- 1983 - Bombing of US Kuwait Embassy - December 12, 1983.

- 1984 - Bombing of US Beirut Embassy - September 20, 1984.

- 1985 - Hijacking TWA Flight 847 hijacked to Beirut - June 14, 1985.

- 1985 - Hijacking cruise ship Achille Lauro - wheelchair-bound American is thrown overboard & killed - October 7, 1985.

- 1986 – Bombing Berlin Disco - frequented by US servicemen April 5, 1986.

- 1988 – Bombing Pan Am Flight 103 – over Lockerbie, Scotland – over 200 murdered - December 21, 1988.

- 1993 – First bombing World Trade Center in New York City, New York City - 7 Killed, 1,042 wounded – February, 26, 1993.

- 1993 – Foiled NY landmarks plot by Omar Abdel Rahman to blow up the Holland and Lincoln tunnels and other New York City landmarks.

- 1993 – Attempted Assassination of President Bush (the older) during visit to Kuwait – April 14, 1993.

- 1994 – Plot to assassinate President Clinton during visit to the Philippines.

- 1995 – Failed Project Bojinka by Ramzi Yousef to blow up a dozen US airliners over the Pacific – end January 1995.

- 1995 – Bombing US military headquarters, Riyadh, Saudi Arabia – November 13, 1995.

- 1996 – Bombing Khobar Towers, Saudi Arabia, housing U.S. foreign military personnel – June 25, 1996.

- 1998 – Bombing US Nairobi Embassy, Kenya, Africa – August 7, 1998.

- 1998 – Bombing US Dar es Salaam Embassy, Tanzania, Africa – August 7, 1998.

- 1999 – Foiled LAX Millennium Plot by Ahmed Ressam to bomb Los Angeles International Airport - Ressam was arrested at US Canadian border.

- 2000 – Failed USS Sullivan's bombing that was taking on fuel in the port of Aden, Yemen – January 3, 2000.

- 2000 – Bombing USS Cole in the port of Aden, Yemen - 17 U.S. Navy sailors murdered – October 12, 2000.

- 2000 - Bombing plaza across from US Manila Embassy – December 30, 2000.

- 2001 – 9/11 Attacks: World Trade Center, Flight 93 and the Pentagon - over 3000 murdered – September 11, 2001.

- 2006 – Fort Hood shootings – Killeen, Texas – 13 killed and wounded 29 others – November 5, 2009.

You read it, now let it sink in. The above list is actions against our nation by Muslims. Islam is a religion with leaders who teach their followers to kill us. Does it make sense to allow people committed to our overthrow to live amongst us? Does it make sense to let them serve inside our military based on their behavior?

The list doesn't even include the Munich Olympic Massacre by a group called Black September. They attacked the Israeli Olympic Village and eventually killed 11 Israeli athletes and coaches and one German Police Officer. Black September was tied to Yasir Arafat's Fatah organization. This took place on the 5th and 6th of September 1972.

Based on the above should we be concerned about Muslims? Let me ask you another question. If your family was attacked over two dozen times by the same breed of dog would you be afraid of that dog? Israel came to the conclusion long ago that there was no reason to punish their citizens and other citizens with serious travel inspections – they just check Muslims. Many of their problems with bombings stopped when they did. We'd rather be politically correct than prudent.

It's a sad world we live in. A worse state of affairs, despite Barack's World Apology Tour, it's not caused by the United States of America. The current problems of security and peace in this world are caused by Muslims, not us. It's not pleasant but it's the truth. Read on.

Ibn Taymiyah, a renowned Muslim philosopher in his book, *The Sword on the Neck of the Accuser of Muhammad* writes, "Believers when in a weakened stage in a non-Muslin country should forgive and be patient with people of the book (meaning Jews and Christians) when they insult Allah and his prophet by any means. Believers should lie to people of the book to protect their lives and their religion."

Does that sound like a group you can trust? Does that sound like a group who will become US citizens and pledge allegiance to our flag? The evidence isn't there to support that position. The evidence says we have a new enemy within and it is Islam. It may very well be communism as well, or a combination of the two. If you love this country you will do your best to see this for yourself. I am just a citizen pissed off that we let this happen. It needs to stop now.

Are the things I am talking about happening right now? Let's take a look around the country.

- The Center for Security Policy recently conducted a study entitled 'Sharia Law and American State Courts. According to Center spokesman David Reaboi, "Islamic demands are now arriving involving cases between foreigners. Sharia enters US Courts when a judge decides to allow the use of say, Pakistani or Saudi family law (Sharia) in a dispute between Pakistani's and Saudi's." It becomes a problem once used because there is then a precedent in our courts.

- Safoorah Khan was a math lab instructor at McArthur Middle School in Berkeley, Illinois for less than a year when she asked for three weeks off to make the hajj. The hajj is a once in a lifetime religious requirement that is one of the five pillars of Islam.

The school district denied the request because she had been there less than a year, it was right before exams, she was the only math instructor available and it violated the union contract that did not provide the same benefit to her infidel counterparts.

The Department of Justice (DOJ) felt differently. The Equal Opportunity Commission made the DOJ aware of the situation and they came in to fix it. They found that the school district was discriminating against Khan because of her religion. The District made a Department of Justice ordered settlement by paying Khan $75,000.00 in damages.

- Muslim students have lodged a complaint against the Catholic University of America, claiming that they are the victims of illegal discrimination because the school does not set aside space for Islamic prayer.

The complaint to the human-rights commission of the District of Columbia is backed by John Banzhaf, a law Professor at nearby George Washington University. A similar action occurred at Trinity University in Texas when Muslim students objected to the words 'in the year of our Lord' on their Diplomas. The complaint was filed by a Muslim convert from Guadalajara, Mexico.

- The Occupy Wall Street movement in Orlando, Florida was found to be supported behind the scenes by a supporter of Hamas and the Muslim Brotherhood.

Tom Trento of the Florida Security Council identifies a lawyer tied to the Muslim Brotherhood and then to Hamas through his association with CAIR, the Council of American Islamic Relations.

Trento reports the evidence is there to show this Muslim man is the driver behind the scenes of the movement.

- A Hyatt hotel in Sugarland, Texas abruptly cancelled a previously scheduled Tea Party event at which an author was scheduled to speak about the dangers of Islam. The hotel was intimidated by threats from none other than, the Council of American Islamic Relations.

Think that it is only happening in our society? What about our churches? Check these reports around the country.

- Social activists involved with an outfit called Faith Shared, a program of Interfaith Alliance and Human Rights First, are trying to promote tolerance and respect of Islam and counter opposition to the Muslim faith. Starting with the National Cathedral in Washington, DC, the message is being spread in churches across America with readings from the Quran.

- Reverend Dr. C. Welton Gaddy, President of Interfaith Alliance said, "The anti-Muslim rhetoric that has pervaded our national conversation recently has shocked and sadden me. Appreciation for pluralism and respect for religious freedom and other human rights are at the core of our democracy. We believe that demonstrating our commitment to those core American values will help counteract the intensified level of negative stereotypes and anti-Muslim bigotry in our recent public discourse."

- Ted Stahnke of Human Rights First said, "With Faith Shared, congregations will send a clear message to the world that Americans respect religious differences and reject bigotry and the demonization of Islam or any other religion.

- This message about the fundamental importance of religious freedom around the world is especially timeless as President Obama prepares to reaffirm the United States support for democracy in the Middle East starting with a speech later this week."

So far over 50 churches across the nation have adopted the practice of preaching from the Quran each week. Is there a precedent for this type of action in the United States? I believe there is.

Universities like Harvard and Yale were founded on Christian principles. The early mottos of Harvard were 'Truth for Christ and the Church' and 'For the Glory of Christ'.

Students were introduced to the schools foundational principles like those found in John 17:3 and Proverbs 2:3. What changed over the years? Professors who were identified as Humanists went to Harvard. Little by little the philosophies changed. You see what those great universities are today. They are Godless. The same principle applies with Islam in the United States today.

And where does our President stand on the Islamic attack. Consider the following.

- The White House recently released a statement from our main man, Barack Hussein Obama. It read:

"Michelle and I extend our greetings for a happy Eid al-Adha to Muslims worldwide and congratulate those performing Hajj.

Thousands of Muslim Americans are among those who have joined one of the world's largest and most diverse gatherings in making the pilgrimage to Mecca and nearby sites.

As Muslims celebrate this Eid, they will also commemorate Abraham's willingness to sacrifice his son by distributing food to those less fortunate around the world. They join the United States and the international community in relief efforts to assist those struggling to survive in the Horn of Africa and those recovering from the devastating earthquake in Turkey.

The Eid and Hajj rituals are a reminder of the shared roots of the worlds Abrahamic faiths and the powerful role that faith plays in motivating communities to serve and stand with those in need.
On behalf of the American people, we extend our best wishes during this Hajj season. Eit Mubarak and Hajj Mabrour."

The ending greeting the President uses means, 'have a blessed festival and may your hajj be accepted.'

- Although representing a country of 210,000,000 Christians as self identified in surveys, the President made no statement on Easter 2011.

- In the Easter 2010 message, in addition to mentioning Christians, Obama included many other religions including Islam in his statement.

- In 2010 the President also offered wishes to the Jews, asking Rabbi's in his message to use their 'moral authority' to stand up for the 'rights' of Muslims.

- On Thanksgiving in 2011 he makes a speech for Thanksgiving that doesn't include the mention of God.

What I find interesting about his statement to Muslims comes a few paragraphs into it. Let me explain a recurring problem with him and the Muslim World.

He said, "They join the United States and the international community in relief efforts to assist those struggling to survive in the Horn of Africa and those recovering from the devastating earthquake in Turkey."

I'm not sure about the earthquake in Turkey, a Muslim country. But let's take a quick look at the Muslim worlds' support for the poor folks in Haiti when an earthquake devastated the capitol city.

The Arab Spring countries of Syria, Libya, Egypt and Iran gave zip, nothing. So why does our President make out like they are big givers? Saudi Arabia keeps a straight face with the west and gave $50 million, a tidy sum.

For the heck of it let's look at a couple of communist countries. Venezuela and Cuba gave zip. Russia tossed over $11 million and China $31 million. Now let's look at the United States contribution. We gave $1.2 billion in aid. Private Citizens and organizations also gave $1.2 billion. The total amount collected from all sources was $3.6 billion. Two thirds of the total came from private sources in the United States. The Muslim world sent 14%, all from the Saudi's. The communists were far less than that amount.

Our President seems to have a need to prop up the Muslim world. He's more in touch with Muslims than he is with his own countrymen. But then again, what evidence is there that he likes America, very little that I could find. And that adds to the concern about our new enemy within.

A follow up to Libya, the country he singlehandedly supported during their 'revolution', is now flying the flag of Al Qaeda over its land in Benghazi.

They have also imposed Sharia Law. Without the help of Barack Obama that would not be the case. He toppled a Dictator and replaced him with a clearer enemy. Our country is in serious trouble. Our enemy Islam has two distinct advantages over us at the present time.

The first advantage is outlined in Mark Steyn's outstanding book *America Alone.* He notes that by sheer birth rates alone, Muslims will outnumber everyone in a matter of years. They're having babies at a rate of 6 to 1 compared to everyone else. At current birth rates America will be the last to be outnumbered. Before we feel good about that, remember, that's like being first in a race of pigs.

The second advantage is what I have been illustrating in the last few bullet points. As with the whole human rights movement, Muslims use our laws against us to change our society. And they're helped along by liberal judges and leaders. We must wake up now.

Do you realize that in 2009 we gave $18 billion dollars in aid to Muslim nations? That is 7 times the aid we gave to Israel. How is it a good idea to finance the very people vowing our destruction? Why would we do that?

Yet, why should we be surprised? Shortly after taking office in 2008, the President gave new direction to NASA. It's Administrator, Charles Bolden spoke on Muslim TV, al-Jazeera. Referring to his new direction from the President he said, "One was he wanted me to help re-inspire children to want to get into science and math; he wanted me to expand our international relationships; and third and perhaps foremost, he wanted me to find a way to reach out to the Muslim world and engage much more with dominantly Muslim nations to help them feel good about their historic contribution to science and math and engineering."

That coming from the man who pulled support for US space flight. The winner from that decision is Russia and China. Then the President sends our head of NASA on a mission to make Muslim kids feel good about their contribution to science. I'm sorry but I call bullshit on that one.

It's important to note that Islam is the only religion known to man that has its very foundation grounded in violence. Their belief is that Muhammad was visited by the Angel Gabriel who called him to be a prophet. As their story goes Muhammad did not want to do it and the Angel Gabriel choked him, not once but on three different occasions.

After the third, he agreed to be the prophet. I think that's important to consider. His followers are blindly committed to his teachings and the teachings of those who followed him. Those teachings include the killing of all infidels, as in you and me.

In Muslim countries around the world today they fund many of their activities by what they call a Jizyah Tax. That is a tax on all infidels living in their country. The tax is for the privilege of living in a Muslim country.

It won't stop there either. In 2010 the Organization of the Islamic Cooperation (OIC) became the largest voting bloc in the UN. They controlled among other things the Human Rights Council. The OIC gets their idea of human rights from what they call the Cairo Declaration. Article 24 reads, "All the rights and freedoms stipulated in this Declaration are subject to the Islamic Shari 'a." How's that for our UN and their Human Rights Council?

As we conclude these remarks regarding our new enemy, I want to double back on some of the communist goals of 1960 and see how they compare. Here is a brief review for you to consider.

The Progress towards the Communist Goals Circa 1960

- US acceptance of coexistence (with the communists) as the only alternative to atomic war.

    ✓ *Do you see any of the President's actions or those of world leaders supporting this goal? Coexistence is very popular on college campuses.*

- US willingness to capitulate in preference to engaging in atomic war.

    ✓ *We don't talk much about Atomic war since the fall of the USSR. But, we do capitulate to the Muslims and the one world government crowd on nuclear disarmament.*

- Develop the illusion that total disarmament by the United States would be a demonstration of moral strength.

    ✓ *Can you see this rhetoric in many phases of American politics these days? Think ... one world government.*

- Permit free trade between all nations regardless of Communist affiliation and regardless of whether or not items could be used for war.

    ✓ *We see this alive and well to the point we now owe China our soul. And one day soon they just may take it. Done!*

- Extension of long term loans to Russia and Soviet satellites.

    ✓ *Water over the bridge at this point. Now we borrow from them. Done!*

- Provide American aid to all nations regardless of Communist affiliation.

    ✓ *You see this in our foreign aid programs to our enemies. We are complete fools on this one. Done!*

- Grant recognition of Red China and its entry into the United Nations.

    ✓ *Done! Note: Our President supports the Palestinian efforts to join the UN. And I happen to agree with Newt Gingrich on this one ... they are a made up people.*

- Prolong conferences to ban atomic tests because the US has agreed to suspend tests as long as negotiations are in progress.

    ✓ *Done!*

- Allow all Soviet satellites representation in the UN.

    ✓ *Done! And remember Palestine is coming if we do nothing.*

- Promote the UN as the only hope for mankind. If its charter is rewritten, demand that it be set up as one-world government with its own independent armed forces.

  ✓ *In process. Think about all the Presidents overtures to the international community and his deferring to the UN on many decisions. The UN is a joke when it comes to peacemaking and governing. Remember Libya was on the Human Rights council.*

- Do away with all loyalty oaths.

  ✓ *Well on the way! Think of the Congressman sworn in on the Quran, not the Bible.*

- Capture one or both of the political parties in the United States.

  ✓ *You make the call? But the Democrats look pretty spot on to me. Do you realize that since 1915 well over 600,000 American fighting men and women lost their lives under Democratic leadership? Under Republicans just over 12,000 lives were lost. Communist activity within our government in World Wars I & II took place under Democratic leadership.*

- Use technical decisions of the courts to weaken basic American institutions by claiming their activities violate civil rights.

  ✓ *Ongoing! There are countless examples today.*

Everything from prayer in schools to allowing Muslims to cover their faces for drivers license photos.

- Get control of the schools. Use them as transmission belts for socialism and current Communist propaganda. Soften the curriculum. Get control of teachers' associations. Put the party line in textbooks.

    ✓ *Done! Look around you. It is well on the way. In Texas a student in a German class who expressed his disbelief in homosexuality was suspended two days and berated by his teacher.*

- Gain control of all student newspapers.

    ✓ *In process! The campuses have long been leaning left. The old line major publications are so left leaning their falling over.*

- Use student riots to foment public protests against programs or organizations which are under Communist attack.

    ✓ *Apply that to Muslim attack? Right now we are experiencing increasing union intervention and violence as well as the Occupy Wall Street movement. Watch for more of the same and an increase in violence here and around the world.*

- Infiltrate the press. Get control of book-review assignments, editorial writing, and policy-making positions.

    ✓ *Hanging by a thread.*

Without Fox News and a few major newspapers this one is done.

In the book The Perfect Spy, *written by Pham Xuan An in 2007, he details his life as the 'Perfect Spy' for the North Vietnamese. He worked for Time Magazine during the war, was educated here thanks to Time and had access to General Westmoreland and all his subordinates.*

His early reports to Hanoi were so accurate that North Vietnamese General Giap said, "We are now in the US war room." Ask yourselves, why would all of this have stopped with the Vietnam War?

- Continue degrading American culture by degrading all forms of artistic expression.

  ✓ *Ongoing! With the constant help of Hollywood's efforts and the ongoing support of the major media outlets, coupled with key liberal courts, our kids don't have a chance today.*

- Control the critics and Directors of art museums.

  ✓ *I've never been in one so I don't have a clue?*

- Eliminate all laws governing obscenity by calling them censorship and a violation of free speech and free press.

  ✓ *Nearly Done. It started with the movements in the 60's. Today, think political correctness and this one is approaching done!*

Also, the ACLU is always on the spot when it comes to attacking American values.

The gay rights movement of today will give way in the next ten years to a movement for recognition of transvestites and then the right of men to have sex with children.

Today, in these United States there is an organization called the North American Man-Boy Love Association (NAMBLA). Its sole purpose is to remove all laws that make sex between a man and a boy, regardless of age, legal. The ACLU supports these efforts. In at least one country in Scandinavia the same organization is now a political party.

- Break down cultural standards of morality by promoting pornography and obscenity in books, magazines, motion pictures, radio and TV.

    ✓ *Think about what we just covered and look around. Color this one done! Check out new TV shows like, Muslim in America and Islamophobia. Hollywood uses programming to drive social issues. You don't see Catholic in America, the Nation's largest single religion. How about Baptist in America?*

- Present homosexuality, degeneracy and promiscuity as normal, natural and healthy.

    ✓ *Done! There is currently an organization known as Gay & Lesbian Alliance against Defamation (GLAD) and another new organization All Out.*

These groups are trying to pressure PayPal to drop the accounts of those they believe are anti-gay.

- Infiltrate the churches and replace revealed religion with social religion. Discredit the Bible and emphasize the need for intellectual maturity which does not need a religious crutch.

  ✓ *In Process! In San Juan Capistrano, California, a couple was fined $300 for holding a weekly Bible Study in their home.*

- Eliminate prayer or any phase of religious expression in the schools on the ground that it violates the principle of separation of church and state.

  ✓ *Done! Yet, teaching Islam as a class is quite fine at the lowest levels of our education system.*

- Discredit the American Constitution by calling it inadequate, old-fashioned, out of step with modern needs, a hindrance to cooperation between nations on a worldwide basis.

  ✓ *In process and being moved along by our current guy in the White House. The schools have been doing this for the last couple decades.*

- Discredit the American Founding Fathers. Present them as selfish aristocrats who had no concern for the common man.

  ✓ *Ongoing! Helped by the ACLU, our schools have been rewriting history for quite some time.*

- Belittle all forms of American culture and discourage the teaching of American history on the ground that it was only a minor part of the big picture.

  ✓ *Ongoing!*

- Support any socialist movement to give centralized control over any part of the culture – education, social agencies, welfare programs, mental health clinics.

  ✓ *Ongoing and being pushed along quickly by Mr. Obama and his Posse'.*

- Eliminate the House Committee on Un-American activities.

  ✓ *Its name was changed in 1969 and 6 years later it was abolished completely. With our growing political correctness there isn't a chance we can say anything about the enemy. Done!*

- Discredit and eventually eliminate the FBI.

  ➤ *Thank God it is still with us by a thread. But you can see the pressure they are under to conform to modern day society.*

- Infiltrate and gain control of more unions.

  ✓ *Ongoing with resurgence under Obama. You don't have to look far to see this happening.*

- Infiltrate and gain control of more big business.

  ✓ *Think George Soros among others. Today we no longer fight countries per se.*

*Companies, drug cartels, religions and some
individuals are more powerful than many countries.
One great example is General Electric. CEO Jeffrey
Immult spends much time in the White House and
enjoys many benefits of doing so.*

- Transfer all the powers of arrest from the police to
  social agencies. Treat all behavioral problems as
  psychiatric disorders which no one but psychiatrists
  can understand or treat.

  > ✓ *In process for sure! Today, there has to be a
  > name for everything, which means if I 'have it'
  > I'm not accountable.*

- Dominate the psychiatric profession and use mental
  health laws as a means of gaining coercive control over
  those who oppose our goals.

  > ✓ *In process for sure! Just read last night where
  > Vladimir Putin, Russia's defiant head of state
  > referred to Senator John McCain as a head case
  > from his time being 'punished' in an Hanoi
  > prison.*

- Discredit the family as an institution. Encourage
  promiscuity and easy divorce.

  > ✓ *Done! The attack on America's family
  > institution is consistent and rigorous and comes
  > from all sides.*

- Emphasize the need to raise children away from the negative influence of parents. Attribute prejudices, mental blocks and retarding of children to suppressive influence of parents.

    ✓ *Ongoing!*

- Create the impression that violence and insurrection are legitimate aspects of the American tradition; that students and special interest groups should rise up and sue a united force to solve economic, political or social problems.

    ✓ *Ongoing with the help of lawyers and judges across this great nation! The violence in the Oakland Occupy Wall Street crowd began a few days after United Steel Workers President Leo Gerard, an Advisor to President Obama said, "I think what we need is, we need more violence."*

- Overthrow all colonial governments worldwide before they are ready for self-government.

    ✓ *Think about the push to pull out of Iraq and Afghanistan long before they are ready for self government. Done!*

- Internationalize the Panama Canal.

    ✓ *Done! Democratic President Jimmy Carter blessed us with this one.*

- Give the World Court jurisdiction over nations and individuals alike.

  ✓ *Ongoing and getting a big push from President Obama.*

That's a lot to think about. The communists are making great headway. Since the 60's they've done quite well. Now that you know that what are you going to do about it?

Considering Obama's World Apology Tour what do the people of the Muslim World think of the United States? The Brookings Institute commissioned what was called the Arab Opinion Poll. The Poll was done in moderate Arab countries like Jordan, Egypt, Lebanon, Morocco, Saudi Arabia and the United Arab Emeritus.

In 2008, at the end of Bush the Younger's reign, the poll found that 83% of those polled had a negative view of the US. They conducted the same poll in 2010 in the same countries and 85% of those polled had a negative view of our country.

Those moderate folks apparently aren't buying what Obama is selling. So who did they say they most admired. Check out this motley list.

1. The Prime Minister of Turkey

2. Hugo Chavez in Venezuela

3. Imanutjob in Iran

4. The head of the terrorist organization Hizb'Allah

5. President of Syria

6. Nicolas Sarkozy, President of France

7. Osama bin Laden

8. Jacques Chirac

9. The Crown Prince of Abu Dhabi

10. Hosni Mubarak formerly head of Egypt

11. The Emir of Dubai

12. Saddam Hussein.

What do you think now? Are you scared yet? You should be. America … we have a problem! Our old enemy is our new enemy and they have surfaced. The Mole was deep for many years but he is now out of the ground. He has a new companion in crime. Let's see what we can do about it?

"The strongest reason for the people to retain the right to keep and bear arms is, as a last resort, to protect themselves against tyranny in government."

Thomas Jefferson

"We have no government armed with power capable of contending with human passions unbridled by morality and religion. Avarice, ambition, revenge, or gallantry, would break the strongest cords of our Constitution as a whale goes through a net. Our Constitution was made only for a moral and religious people. It is wholly inadequate to the government of any other."

John Adams

Wake Up America! The Enemy's Within!

My wife has read parts of the manuscript for this book as I wrote it. She says, "Ed, you're depressing me! You're scaring me". That's exactly what I hoped to do. When we were overrun by the enemy in Vietnam, someone would scream, "They're inside the wire!" Being overrun is really, really scary. I never dreamed I'd be screaming 'they're inside the wire' stateside nearly five decades after the war! But they are fighting from inside and its real. It's time to whack the Mole out of our country for good!

One of the major problems America has today can be summed up with a line Jack Nicholson made famous in the movie *A Few Good Men*. He said, when being cross examined about the truth, "You can't handle the truth!" As a citizen of this great nation I've worked hard to lay out the truth and tell you exactly where our great nation is headed today.

The first truth is that our President is a dangerous man. He is leading America down a path we, as a people, do not intend to go. The tough thing is not what we know about him that is troubling. It is what we don't know about him. Can you handle that truth? You must.

A nation or family that loses its history will lose its way. We have a President of the United States of America who dislikes the country he was chosen to lead. He said so. His wife said so. Under his leadership our once proud nation is becoming but a slight image of its former self.

My Brit friend, a very successful business person in Canada said, "America has been the engine for freedom, economics and entrepreneurialism since its inception. What is going on down there?" Everyone wonders about America except the majority of Americans.

We must realize that communism, the enemy of democracy's worldwide, is alive and well and inside of America. It did not die with the fall of the Berlin Wall as most Americans thought. It is deeply imbedded in our political process.

Along with communism we have a new enemy and it is Islam. We have a string of history in the form of acts of war against America to prove it. They have announced they are out to destroy us. They work very hard at bringing about our destruction. They now have a US President supporting them.

Our Marxist President is the finishing pitcher in the game of taking America to Socialism. Is he a Muslim? I don't know. What we do know is that he favors Islam over Christianity. I also know a communist would make an alliance with anyone to get what they want; and a Muslim would do likewise. Somewhere in there lies the truth about Barack Hussein Obama.

I know that at some point our enemies merged their attack on America for a common purpose. That purpose is to gain world dominance. One of them must lose. But if you look at their ideology, one is atheist and one is for Allah, they both think it won't be them.

Our current President has displayed, beyond a shadow of a doubt, that he is anti-American. He has displayed that he is a Socialist with a Socialist agenda. He has also displayed that he is a supporter of Islam. He is either a Muslim or a Godless communist. Pick you poison. Either one will kill us. He is the one selected to usher in the end of America as we know it. We must stop him in 2012.

Why haven't we seen this before? We have it too good. We forgot our history. We don't even teach it in school. The liberals have stolen the lessons of the Civil War, the awful one that was fought at home.

They've taken the history of World War I, World War II, Korea, and Vietnam and what those sacrifices meant to the free world. They portray our current wars in the Gulf War, Iraq and Afghanistan to make us out to be war mongers.

They have done it so well today that the only ones fighting the wars in Iraq and Afghanistan are the servicemen and women and their families and extended community's, no one else. You rarely see a report on the major networks about what is or isn't happening in the War on Terror. That is until Obama engages us in another Muslim war, like Libya. The one we had no business in, but we find Anderson Cooper right on the spot, promoting the Presidents agenda.

Obama ran on a platform of change. Then he brought in his commie cohorts and his Czars to help push that change. Digest what is in this book. How do you like the change he has brought us? He wants to change America into what he thinks it should be. He wants a Socialist nation, not the one our Founding Fathers intended for us in America.

Let's take a final look at one of the big collaborators in this plan to change America. The media, which was once full of independent journalists, is today a laughing stock of what it once was. The move to media empires has destroyed independent news. They've also become promoters for their candidate. They're biased. Don't think so? Listen to some comments by a respected Canadian journalist, Rex Murphy of CBC.

In an article entitled 'The American Media: Failure's Maidservants" Murphy says, "As bad as the economic news continues to emanate from the United States - with a double-dip recession now all but certain - a reckoning is overdue. American journalism will have to look back at the period starting with Barrack Obama's rise, his assumption of the presidency and his conduct in it to the present, and ask itself how it came to cast aside so many of its vital functions?

In the main, the establishment American media abandoned its critical faculties during the Obama campaigning - and it hasn't reclaimed them since." Think hard about this one. Fox News isn't offering this observation; it is a prominent journalist living in our neighbor to the north. He goes on to say, "Much of the Obama coverage was orchestrated sycophancy. They glided past his pretensions - when did a presidential candidate before 'address the world' from the Brandenburg gate in Berlin? They ignored his arrogance".

Stop and think about that for a minute? America is guilty of letting the media get away with Obama's facade. The ignored what we don't know about him. The promoted a man with zero qualifications. They helped him get elected President of the world's beacon of freedom. His first act is to immediately begin to turn off the light that guides the free world. The media stands by and ignores it.

Mr. Murphy comments further, "The media walked right past the decades-long association of Obama with the weird and racist Pastor Jeremiah Wright. In the brief storm over the issue, one CNN host - inexplicably - decided that CNN was going to be a 'Wright-free-zone'. He could have hung out a sign: No bad news about Obama here". Again, think about what he said. He is Canadian for goodness sakes. He's no right wing nut job or radio host. He is an outside observer. We must throw Obama out in 2012!

Did you ever wonder how Mr. Obama moved the Clinton Machine aside during the Democratic Campaign in 2008? The article by Mr. Murphy makes several points about how Hillary got moved aside. Everyone but Obama got viciously attacked and our media was derelict in their duty to the truth and impartiality. Does that remind you of what has happened to Herman Cain? Mr. Cain ran for the Georgia Senate and not a word of the sexist allegations came forward. But this time his challenger is Mr. Obama. Think about it!

Our Canadian journalist ends by saying, "As a result, the press gave the great American republic an untried, unknown and, it is becoming more and more frighteningly clear, incompetent figure as President. Under Obama, America's foreign policies are a mixture of confusion and costly impotence. It is increasingly bypassed or derided; the great approach to the Muslim world, symbolized by the Cairo speech, is in tatters. Its debt and deficits are a weight on the entire global economy. And the office of the presidency is less and less a symbol of strength".

He continues, "To the degree the press neglected its function as watchdog and turned cupbearer to a Styrofoam demigod, it is partner in the flaws and failures of what is turning out to be one of the most miserable performances in the modern history of the American presidency".

He is exactly right. We no longer have a free press. We Americans need to make it change and do its duty or quit participating in the charade called 'the news'. Remember, one of the key principles of communism was to take our freedom of the press. Take the radio station.

Does America matter anymore? Mr. Murphy and many others think so. I've yet to hear of anyone dying on the ocean to get anywhere else.

A few years back I was flying from Peoria, Illinois to Chicago O'Hare. Prior to take off from Peoria I was doing a phone interview about my book *Dead Center*. When we arrived in O'Hare and deplaned I was approached by a passenger who sat in front of me.

He asked if I was an Author. I said yes. He said he wanted to write a book but didn't think that he could. He then stood for twenty-five minutes telling me of the story of how he came to America.

He was Cuban and his father sent him and his brother to American families when the Castro Revolution succeeded. He told me he went to a family in Kansas City while his brother went to Minneapolis. He told me how hard it was because neither one spoke English. For several years his brother thought he was the only Cuban left on the planet. I can't imagine, can you?

He was a distinguished gentleman. With tears in his eyes he told me what happened to his parents. He told me how bad it is under Castro. He told me how he loved America. We parted friends, he with tears in his eyes, me with a large lump in my throat for what America has and no longer appreciates.

We must get in touch with our history. We're certainly a country with problems, areas in need of improvement and change. But we are much better than we used to be. As I told my kids as they grew up, "We've got problems, but we're way ahead of second place."

Let's take a quick look at Europe, Obama's model for America's future. Europe today, the place Obama wants to model, followed our lead in banking. When we collapsed they did also. "Europe is in danger", said Polish Finance Minister Jacek Rostowski, whose country currently chairs EU meetings. He then said, "If the Euro Zone breaks up, the European Union will not survive". It is no longer just us.

Greece looks like they may be the first to go. It is nearing default on many of its loans. When the Greek Prime Minister George Papandreou tried to take the reins of his country, rioters hit the streets. Why? One reason was because the government was going to have to reduce expenses. It's a novel idea certainly, but a shock to the people in Greece. Greek workers can retire at 50 years old.

That is one among many idiotic socialist ideas that the government will take care of you from cradle to grave. That's the model Obama wants for America. It's working well in Europe with Italy, Spain, France, and the Netherlands joining Greece with deep trouble.

The one world government movement in Europe just might make a move forward soon. Driven by the serious debt crisis in Europe, they're considering some downright socialist changes. To save the Euro here are a couple ideas under consideration.

One idea gaining momentum is a radical proposal in which countries that use the common currency would cede control of a big chunk of their budgets to a central authority. Some say the proposal would be a big leap toward a United States of Europe, a move that could greatly enhance European stability, but at the cost, critics say, of national sovereignty and democratic accountability.

Another plan being aired in the face of fierce German resistance is for the Euro zone's six triple-A rated nations to pool their resources through a joint bond to prop up some of the single currency bloc's most indebted members. Germany, the EU's richest member, rejects the idea because it fears it would be tapped for the lion's share of the bailout.

President Obama, speaking after a meeting with the European Union's leaders said, "If Europe is contracting, or if Europe is having difficulties, then it's much more difficult for us to create good here jobs at home." Hide your pocketbook folks, Obama is about to hit the debt throttle again!

Let's take one last look at the Middle East, and how our New President is doing over there:

- Let's check out the head of the beast, Iran. A recent headline read, "*US Envoy Blasts Iran's Nuclear 'Deceit'.*"

It tells of US Secretary of Energy, Steven Chu, blasting Iran for denial, deceit and evasion in refusing to open its nuclear program to an increase in outside overview. I have one big question. What planet is Steven Chu from? Did he not get the memo over the past twenty years or so about Iran's very consistent deceit? How about their denouncement of Israel and the US? Of course Mr. Obama, the world's greatest negotiator and community organizer, said he is going to negotiate a deal with the devil.

- Obama sends messages to the Muslim world almost daily. Obama's latest Muslim message is his decision to recognize and meet with none other than - The Muslim Brotherhood. There has been a ban in this country on diplomatically recognizing the Muslim Brotherhood since 1954. But it's okay now, due to the 'Arab Spring' and the fact that in recent Egyptian elections the Brotherhood won over the supposed 'driving force' of young people candidates by a mere 78% for the boys from the 'hood, and 22% for the reformers.

- In his infinite wisdom, Mr. President thinks it best to put an end to a 57 year ban on these folks. Back then, when the ban was established, they weren't even calling us The Great Satan. They weren't even proclaiming they wanted to kill us all as infidels. The Wisdom of Barry Soetoro, aka Barack Hussein Obama is amazing, fascinating, and very frightening as well as deceitful.

Veteran Chicago Tribune columnist and distinguished member of its editorial board, Steve Chapman has an article titled, *"Why Obama Should Withdraw"*. Wow!

He wrote it on the 19th of September in 2011. The article is for real. Not only that – he says Hillary should run instead. Chapman suggested Obama's 2012 campaign slogan should be, "Midnight in a Coal Mine". Ouch! That's gotta' hurt.

His article is surprising coming out of Chicago. Hopefully more people will see the man behind the mask. He keeps himself before the camera. I don't know if you happened to be watching TV when the President was giving his speech on his latest $447 billion stimulus package. He stands proudly on TV, the Brent Spence Bridge spanning the Ohio River between Ohio and Kentucky in the background. We both know Ohio and Kentucky are key battleground states in the 2012 election but this is a business trip.

The President proudly discusses the bridge and how it needs repair. He implies these are the types of projects his stimulus package will support. After all, it's one of the busiest trucking routes in America.

What he failed to mention was that his jobs bill is for immediate projects. Another miss was the fact the bridge doesn't need immediate repair. He failed to say there's already a plan for a new $2.3 billion bridge across the Ohio River at that very point.

He further failed to mention the new bridge is not scheduled to start construction for about 4 years and there is not a completion date yet. My goodness, we put a man on the moon in less time than that.

Do you think maybe his speech writer screwed up, or maybe an autumn glare of the afternoon sun hit his teleprompter? Or maybe, just maybe, he is lying every time his lips move.

Do you see the charades our President plays? When it comes to the economy he has some real funny math for a guy from Harvard. By his own admission at a private fundraiser in late September, the jobs he is going to create will only cost $239,236 per job. Does that bother you?

I skipped a lot of school and math isn't my strong suit but doesn't that number just scream stupidity? I mean if we just paid about 1.9 million people, say $240,000 in a lump sum, then kept half of that in taxes - well, we'd be a lot better off. Can't these folks do the math?

We've previously discussed concern over Obama and states' rights. I discovered a little treasure hidden deep inside the American Jobs Act. That's the name of the President's stimulus package. His 'Act' says on Page 133:

- Section 376: FEDERAL AND STATE IMMUNITY.

  a. Abrogation of State Immunity - A State shall not be immune under the 11th Amendment to the Constitution from a suit brought by a Federal Court of competent jurisdiction for a violation of this Act. (Think about this now - really hard, it gets even better.)

  b. (A) WAIVER - A States receipt or use of Federal financial assistance for any program or activity of a State 'shall constitute a waiver of sovereign immunity, under the 11th Amendment to the Constitution or otherwise, to a suit brought by an employee or applicant for employment of that program or activity under this Act for a remedy authorized under Section 375 (C) of this Act.

I have to admit here I haven't been privy to all that fancy book learning. I'm also not one of those high classed lawyers; although I did once take a correspondence law course I read about on a matchbook. It was from Chicago's prestigious LaSalle University Law School. I even won my first and only case against Manufacturers Bank of Detroit. I think that might put me with a better record than the President. I've read he's never tried a case himself.

In these two sections of the Obama stimulus package the law above as written simply says, if the state takes any money from the fed's stimulus package they are thereby giving up their state sovereignty. Slick, eh?

The 'Act' is another underhanded attempt by the Obama Administration to revoke states rights and give the Fed's more power. I don't have to go to Occidental College, Columbia, Harvard or even LaSalle Extension to know whether this is okay ... hell no, it's not!

As I quoted Willie before, "That shit ain't right!" It takes us one more step closer to socialism. We're on a deep decline and sliding like our ass is on fire - because it is! We must act now!

Many years ago while working in Corporate America, one of my peers gave me an award for 'asking questions no one has answers for' for five consecutive years. He was right. I've been asking them since Vietnam and will to the day I die. We must act now! I cannot emphasize that enough. If we don't, we'll wake up and be sliding down the abyss and over the cliff with our asses burning out like a shooting star.

* * *

We also need to look at Obama in regards to his stand on education. Today, the government has our children and we must take them back. If we reelect this guy we'll lose the future, the one we owe our kids and grandkids.

Let's talk about State's rights and education. Senator Marco Rubio of Florida urged our Education Secretary to obey the Constitution. The background is President Obama ordering his underling, Arne Duncan, to reauthorize the No Child Left Behind legislation. The bill before the legislature is 600 pages and costs $25 billion. That of course is a rounding error using Obama math.

Rubio's problem is that Obama wanted the bill passed by the opening of the school year, and Congress didn't get it done. When the bill wasn't passed Obama moved key parts of the bill forward without the authority to do so. He used 'waivers' signed by his Education Secretary, Arne Duncan.

Using waivers is okay for items already in place, but not for legislation not yet passed. The Administration is issuing 'conditional waivers' requiring the states who take the money to abide by the administrations changes. As outlined in the legislation noted above. Emperor Obama has spoken, to hell states' rights.

Speaking of the Department of Education, look at what Indiana schools are doing. They're no longer teaching writing in their public schools. It appears to be a trend, other cities like Winchester, Virginia are following suit.

Yep, from the Hoosiers of today on, there will be no more penmanship or longhand to get in the way of a good education. They're tossing it out in favor of typing skills. I learned both in school, but our Department of Education apparently knows best. I sure hope Quicken Loans takes over 100% of the market, because for our Hoosiers in Indiana, they'll at least be able to sign their mortgages electronically. Remember, one of the communist goals was to undermine our education system. Think they have succeeded?

One way they succeed is through consolidation. In 1940 America had 120,000 school boards. That is a tall order for the fed's to control. Today there are 15,000 school boards and a massive Department of Education. We are quietly being moved to socialism.

Sure hope you're awake and prepared to stop our slide, my butts getting really hot. Our country depends on it. We owe it to our children and grand and great grand children. We owe it to the world. We must throw out socialism and Obama. We must do it now.

- When Obama took office the unemployment rate was 6.8%. The latest figure is 9.1%. That's after spending a fortune in bail outs and stimulus money.

- During Obama's time in office the national debt has risen by 50%. It's still climbing.

- Consumer spending has dropped by 30%.

- A mere two years after the administration announced its 'Recovery Summer', 68% of Americans polled think things are getting worse. That figure is 11% higher than on last Election Day.

- 57% of the American people do not believe the recovery has even started yet.

- Obama announces the withdrawal of all troops from Iraq just as he begins his reelection campaign. Expect most troops out of Afghanistan right before next year's election too.

Understand, both withdrawals are premature, and many of those countrymen are going to die soon after we leave, just like Vietnam. Both countries will be back in the enemy's hands within months of withdrawal.

If all of that doesn't move your needle to the right, consider our national security and Mr. Obama.

Muslim groups such as the Council on American Islamic Relations (CAIR) and its close cousin, the Muslim Public Affairs Council (MPAC) issued formal complaints about American law enforcement training materials. These are the materials the FBI uses and trains law enforcement with throughout the country.

Unless the US government removes negative references to Islam or Muslims from the FBI's training material, Salam al-Marayati, President of MPAC said that Muslims in America will no longer cooperate with the FBI. And, al-Marayati demanded a clear, unequivocal apology from the FBI for the offensive materials. He also demanded that the FBI establish a thorough and transparent vetting process in selecting its trainers and materials. How do you like that? Did you hear that on the nightly news?

What did our President do? Did he put them in their place? Did he support the Federal Bureau of Investigation? Well, no he didn't. He has ordered that all materials used by the law enforcement and national security communities be pulled back. They must eliminate all references to Islam that some Muslim groups claim are offensive. That's a fact!

A spokesman for Attorney General Eric Holder said, "I want to be perfectly clear about this: training materials that portray Islam as a religion of violence or with a tendency towards violence are wrong, they are offensive, and they are contrary to everything that this president, this attorney general and Department of Justice stands for. They will not be tolerated."

We should have had a clue when our new President, shortly after taking office said, "Words matter … because one of the ways we're going to win this struggle ["war on terror"] is through the battle of [Muslims'] hearts and minds." The brackets are there to give emphasis to what he was really saying. He is the enemy within.

The censorship within the military and homeland security departments is criminal. In last year's Quarterly Defense Report (QDR), a strategic document, there is not a single mention of anything remotely related to Islam. The document actually stresses climate change, which it says is an accelerant of instability and conflict around the world.

- Does that frighten you?

To what lengths and depths will Obama go to achieve victory in 2012? He has already boasted that he will spend $1 billion on his reelection campaign. Does he have friends who are helping? You bet he does. Hollywood is just one example.

There is a new movie in the makings to the tune of about $75 million. That's chump change for Obama and his minions. It is based on the raid by Navy Seals that resulted in the killing of Osama bin Laden.

That in itself is not surprising, right? The movie is now scheduled to open on October 12, 2012. As you know if you do the math that is just four weeks before the 2012 election. I bet we can be certain it will make Obama look cool and certain in his fight for right.

Not so fast though, check this out. The Director is Kathryn Bigelow. She also directed the movie *Hurt Locker* based on IED teams in Iraq. The problem comes when a Director is given government access to secret military information, the Director must have approval for every single scene depicted in the movie.

Kathryn Bigelow violated that agreement when filming and producing *Hurt Locker*. In the past when a Director or writer violated their written agreement with the Pentagon they were denied future access for future projects. In Ms. Bigelow's case, she's been granted almost unlimited access for the filming of the bin Laden picture. Why do you think that is?

Maureen Dowd reported that "the moviemakers are getting top level access to the most classified mission in history." Why do you suppose they have been given such access to a sensitive mission?

Navy Admiral Eric Olsen said, "the raid that killed bin Laden was successful because nobody talked about it before, and if we want to preserve this capability nobody better talk about it after." That fact apparently has fallen on the deaf ears of our Commander in Chief. Reelection is much more important than preserving military capability.

The movie is being released through Sony, who has final say in the release date. Sony recently hosted a gala fundraiser at its studios in California. Doesn't seem so bi-partisan anymore does it?

Representative Peter King of New York who chairs the House Homeland Security Committee wrote a letter to the Department of Defense and CIA demanding to know, whether the movie will be reviewed before its release and whether the identity of undercover agents and other sensitive information revealed to the moviemakers will be disclosed. So far, he's the only one questioning what is going. It appears to be politics as usual.

You may be thinking we could never get an 'enemy within' here in the United States? Do you think a Trojan Horse couldn't become President of the United States? Think again.

The 1971 book *The Shattered Silence* is for you. It's the story of an Israeli agent by the name of Eli Cohen. It is a fascinating story of a 14 year old boy selected to work his way into the Syrian government and become its head of defense. It took him nearly four decades but he was in place to be named the next Deputy Minister of Defense for Syria when he was discovered.

However, he wasn't discovered until he had passed information on to Israel enabling them to launch a preventive strike against the Arab Nations and ultimately win the Six Day War in 1967. Eli Cohen was hung on national TV in Syria. It has happened before and it can and it has happened today.

The time is now! It's not time for us to be positive or negative. It's not time for us to be Liberal or Conservative. It's not time for us to be Republican or Democrat. It's time for us to get real and be Americans and do what is right!

I don't know how many of you saw the movie *Planes, Trains and Automobiles*. The greatest scene in the comedy is when stars John Candy and Steve Martin are driving in a car at night when they fall asleep. They awake on the wrong side of the Interstate heading straight between two oncoming eighteen wheelers.

As they pass between the two semis, sparks flying on both sides of their car, they scream as if being eaten alive by lions. Their bodies turned to skeletons as the big rigs crunch by. We are them right now. We're being eaten alive and we better start screaming and do something about it. The time to act is now!

"If we desire to avoid insult, we must be able to repel it;
if we desire to secure peace, one of the most powerful instruments
of our rising prosperity, it must be known, that we are at all times
ready for War."

George Washington

Actions We Must Take Now

Our President won the election by preaching hope and change. Hope is a belief in something I cannot see. Our President, his hidden supporters and his socialist staff see the change he is planning. The American people as a whole do not.

Change on the other hand is about behavior. I have shared the last couple hundred pages of his planned changes with you. Now, let's look at what you can do about it. Remember the quote I shared earlier, "What we do every day is what we believe, all the rest is just talk". It's time for all of us to do something!

National Level Actions:

- OBAMA MUST BE VOTED OUT IN 2012!

  You have seen the evidence. Our President is working for a Socialist America in the very least. He is either a closet Muslim, which I believe, or an atheist who uses whatever he needs to reach his goals. Those goals are in line with the goals of the American Communist Party USA. The bankrupting of America is part of the plan, not a result of his incompetence. If we do not accomplish this number-one action of voting him out, the following actions will be irrelevant. We are that far along in the move towards making America a socialist state.

- WE MUST GET OTHERS OUT TO VOTE OBAMA OUT OF OFFICE!

  You must spread the word to others about the truth America faces today. Let's make a goal.

Get at least five people into the cause of voting Obama from office. You must, our nation depends on it.

- WE MUST THEN SHOW OUR VOTES IN CONGRESS!

  Many in Congress, either by intention or ignorance; are socialists. We must vote out the socialists (Pelosi, Reed, Frank and many, many more) in Congress. The Socialists and the Incompetents must go. And that is probably 80-90% of the bunch.

- WE MUST CHANGE THE LAWS IN CONGRESS!

  In the least we must change the following:

  1. We must have term limits on all members of Congress. I am convinced beyond a shadow of a doubt that our Founding Fathers never intended for us to be led by professional politicians. Term limits should be one term of 4 years for the House of Representatives and 6 for the Senate. When the changeover takes place everyone with 4 or 6 years in office is out.

  2. We must enact laws in Congress that they can pass no bill that does not apply to every American. That means that either Congress is covered by Social Security or we are covered by their plans. Either way, it is a one way street. All for one and one for all. In every aspect of the bills they pass.

  3. In keeping with 'b' above, the laws will be changed that no one in government gets a pass when it comes to insider trading. Today, Congress is a business, and it pays well. That must stop.

4. We must demand the Federal government respect and honor states rights. They must get out the business of telling states what to do. They must respect the Constitution as it was originally written. That is, we are a Republic.

5. Being a member of Congress cannot be a full time job. It is a service we are willing to give for our country for a defined period of time. Think how often we hear Senator so and so just retired after 50 years of service to our country. I understand service to be something I give with no expectation of a return. Mother Teresa gave the world a wonderful service in her life. Senator Byrd and Senator Kennedy for instance, did not. They were rewarded handsomely for the business of Congress; the retirement they receive is early, lavish and embarrassing. It must stop.

6. We must place the job of a member of Congress in their home district offices. They travel to Washington, not from Washington. Their work should be with their constituents, not talking incessantly in DC. It would also make lobbying much more difficult.

7. We must get involved with our members of Congress. When something is important or they do something stupid, we need to let them know. Use the phone, email, letter writing or visit their offices. Make your voice heard to take back America.

8. We must write letters to the editor of your local newspapers expressing the view of what is happening to our country.

If they do not respond, write anyway and insist your voice be heard. Then write a letter to the editor telling the public they did not respond.

9. Write and call your local radio and TV stations when you hear national level news that is not in keeping with a free America.

Local Level Actions:

- WE MUST ELECT GOVERNORS WHO REPRESENT AMERICA AND THE CONSTITUTION!

  The power in our process needs to be at the state and local levels. We need Governors who are going to stand up and be counted when it comes to our rights. We need more Governors like we have in Ohio, South Carolina, Texas, Wisconsin and Arizona.

- WE MUST ELECT MAYORS OF OUR CITIES WHO REFLECT AMERICAN VALUES AS INTENDED BY THE CONSTITUTION!

  Many of our cities are currently led by socialists. We must get involved and stop the bleeding before it is too late. Hold them accountable with your votes.

- WE MUST GET INVOLVED IN LOCAL POLITICS AND ENSURE WE HAVE LEADERS IN PLACE WHO SUPPORT AMERICA!

  We can no longer sit back and allow incompetents and socialists into office anywhere. The time has come to wake up, stay awake and get involved.

- WE MUST GET INVOLVED IN OUR SCHOOLS AND BOARD OF EDUCATIONS!

  The war for socialism and communism starts with the education system. They are well on their way to achieving their goals. The liberals have a strong foothold today in our schools. We must do all we can to change that, and fast. Get involved in your school boards and make a difference.

Family Level Actions:

The family is the most basic organization of life on earth. It is in the family that values and morals must be taught. The society around us must then reflect and support those values. That is no longer the case today. The family is under attack from all sides. That attack has been subtle but effective. We are now facing the extinction of the American family.

We are in the midst of a major crisis. One of the key Marxist/Communist goals is to destroy the family. They are winning right now. It is a crisis of family. If we do not take charge of this situation our future is not in doubt, it is sealed to doom. Our families are under attack by our news media, the television and movie industry, our schools, our judges and our government. Do you see this as a problem? You must do something about it now.

Here are a few actions you must take …

- WE MUST TAKE CHARGE OF OUR FAMILIES AND MAKE THEM IMPORTANT IN OUR LIVES!

  ❖ Spend time with your family. On your death bed, work will not be important, only family.

- ❖ Take your family to church, don't send them.

- ❖ Teach your family the power of faith and prayer.

- ❖ Understand that raising children is 90% love and 10% discipline.

- ❖ Teach your family the truth about America and its history and what America means to the world.

- ❖ Listen to your children and what they're being taught in school. If it is not to your liking and not in keeping with American values make your voice heard. Talk to the school, the leaders and the media if necessary. If that doesn't work go to the Internet.

- ❖ It is up to parents to make sure children understand there is a purpose for education. That purpose is to make them productive, self sufficient human beings. You must give them both roots and wings.

- ❖ Teach your children to be leaders and not followers. By your example teach them correct principles and they will in fact govern themselves.

- ❖ Teach your children that the government exists to protect its citizens and manage issues that cross state lines. It does not exist to take care of them from cradle to grave.

- ❖ Teach your children that the government produces nothing. Its entire income is received from its citizens and its citizens businesses and corporations. What the government gives it must first take.

❖ Teach your family that America is a Judea-Christian nation. It is founded on Biblical principles. You must lead by example demonstrating those principles with your family if you want to make a difference.

❖ Teach your family that our country was built on immigrants. Immigrants that came and want to be part of what America is.

❖ Teach them tolerance for all people and religions. Also, teach them that the tolerance stops when those people want to change and stomp on American values.

We've covered many miles of information in this book. Most of it is very controversial. The key is – it's all true. I hope you're awake. I hope and pray you're moved to action.

When I was consulting in the business world and was charged with turning an operation around, I would first ask myself two questions relating to why things were so screwed up.

➢ **Is it a deficiency of knowledge?**

Or

➢ **Is it a deficiency of execution?**

In this case it is a little of both. I have tried, through extensive research, to give you what one pissed-off American found. I found evidence our President is supporting our Muslim enemy and streaking us towards socialism. Study it, digest it and you now have the knowledge. To turn this operation we call America around – we must now execute. When we lose the flame of freedom and liberty it will be much more difficult to light it again.

START EXECUTING BY DECIDING TO DO SOMETHING. THE FIRST THING TO DO IS VOTE OUR SOCIALIST PRESIDENT OUT OF OFFICE IN 2012. IF WE DON'T DO THAT, THE REST WILL NO LONGER MATTER.

Once we have him out of office, together, we can start on the rest of the problems outlined in our action list. The time is now or never. I hope you're with me! Our Founding Fathers did not establish this great country for us to let it get away.

WE MUST ACT, AND WE MUST ACT NOW!

"All it takes for Evil to Triumph is for Good Men to do nothing"

Edmund Burke

Acknowledgements

I'd like to first thank God and His Son, Jesus Christ for the opportunity to live in the United States of America. I am grateful for the life I've been permitted to live.

I have to thank Him for my wife who has put up with me for over forty three years and counting. The last year while researching, assembling and writing this book, she has been extremely patient, understanding and supportive of the time it has taken to complete.

I thank my kids for putting up with me and my antics for their entire lives. I pray they might read this and be moved to action in helping save this great country.

I offer this work for my grandchildren and their posterity. If we do not make changes and make them right away, my grandchildren and yours will have no chance to have the future we have all enjoyed. May we save America for all those following us?

I'm thankful to the United States Marine Corps for making me into the person I am today. I'm thankful for the opportunity to have fought for my country. And to all those wonderful Marines I have had the pleasure of serving and fighting with, as well as my young Marine friends today … Semper Fidelis.

I'm grateful to my friends and supporters. Thanks for believing in me. To my wife's best friends from high school, the U-Crew, I offer my sincere thanks. While you wondered about me for years, you've been great friends and supporters. I've felt a growing need to do something for the past couple of years. Obamunism is the product of that feeling. It is all true. I wondered at first, who am I to write such a book? Then I decided, I am an American, a Father, a Grandfather, and a Veteran. I am also thoroughly pissed off at what's happening to my country. That's qualifications enough.

*"However political parties may now and then answer
popular ends, they are likely in the course of time and things,
to become potent engines, by which cunning, ambitious,
and unprincipled men will be enabled to subvert
the power of the people and to usurp for themselves
the reins of government, destroying afterwards
the very engines which have lifted them to unjust dominion."*

George Washington
Farewell Address, September 17, 1796

Authors Note

I know many of the things you've read in here are shocking. I also know they are true and felt it was something I should share in the hope of causing at least a small ripple in the pool of life in America.

There will be many people who will take exception to the things I've shared and that is their right to do so. For that reason I'd like to close this work with three messages I think are important.

1. First, you won't find the usual footnotes and references found in the back of most books. I have the sources for all my comments but I am not sharing until our President chooses to share the critical parts of his background that none of us know. If he doesn't have to share, then I don't either.

2. Secondly, when you meet a true liberal you will not be able to discuss the items in this book. They will be angry and denounce it offhand. They will then say I don't have any knowledge to write such a book. Since I don't provide my sources will add more fuel to their fire. I personally think that 80% of those supporting Obama do not understand his real direction and 20% are true and blind supporters.

3. Third, many will question my Christian faith and my comments on Islam. For those folks I see no conflict. Christ preached peace and when he came he fulfilled the Old Testament and brought us a new law in the New Testament. Islam does not preach peace.

Love is a willingness to sacrifice for the spiritual growth of another person. Christ preached love for all, including our enemies. Islam does not. When raising children we pay attention to who they are around and how they are behaving. When your child has a friend who preaches hate, tortures animals and likes to hit your child – you sever ties. Islam cannot for they preach it.

Evil is that which is damaging to our soul. Christ preached against evil. The actions of Islam against America are evil. A long distance mentor of mine is the late Jim Rohn. Jim said, "It is not important why a person sold out to evil, it is only important that you carve them out of your life".

We need to carve Islam out of America until which time as they prove they want to be part of America, like nearly all immigrants who have preceded them. That is not discrimination, or anti-Christian behavior, that is common sense. We must not forget that Christ tossed the money changers from the Temple.

In this book I have only tried to pull the fire alarm and ring the bell of distress for a country I love. We must understand that the 2012 election is the most important election in the history of America. I don't know if we can turn the country around even if we vote Obama out of office. But I do know we cannot turn it around if he gets a second term – our end will be official at that point.

Give us a chance … vote in 2012 to toss Barack Hussein Obama out of office. Then we can try and work on the rest of the problems and people in Washington!

Ed Kugler - Author

About the Author

Ed has been called a Renaissance man and some other things not printable. One CEO even named him his Senior Vice President of Truth. His greatest award is from his peers at Frito Lay when they gave him the award for 'Five Consecutive Years of Asking Questions Our Leaders Won't Answer'. He is known to say things others are only thinking.

He learned his early lessons as a young man, a Marine Sniper, while serving two years in the Vietnam War. He is the Author of *Dead Center – A Marine Snipers Two Year Odyssey in the Vietnam War*. Ed returned from the war where he worked as a truck driver, mechanic, dispatcher and eventually General Manager of a small trucking company.

After ten years in trucking Ed joined Frito Lay where he was promoted five times in six years and spent thirteen years there before transferring to Pepsi Cola where he became Director of Distribution. After three years he left PepsiCo to become Vice President of Worldwide Logistics for Compaq Computer. His last real job was Senior Vice President of Operations and Quality for Telxon Corporation.

He left Corporate America in 1998 to get his life back. He established Direct Hit, a change and operational turnaround company where he served companies like DHL, Pepsi Cola, PepsiAmericas, APL, General Bottlers, Ropak Southwest, Schlumberger, Exel Logistics, Restoration Hardware, Caterpillar and many more.

Ed has been a frequent guest speaker to the US Marine Corp, the US Army Scout Sniper Association, the Alaska Governors Conference, the Colorado District of Attorneys Association and many corporations across America. He is retired today and continues writing books.

He is the father of three, grandfather to four and has been married to his wife Gloria for forty three years and counting.

Do we really believe George Washington bravely crossed the Delaware for a mutual fund?

Rabbi Schmuley Boteach

"Did Revolutionary War troops walk barefoot in the frozen wasteland of Valley Forge in the hope that they would eventually wear Ferragamo loafers?"

Rabbi Schmuley Boteach